THE ENCYCLOPEDIA OF VERY IMPORTANT EVENTS THROUGH MODERN HISTORY

54 Earth-Shattering Events That Changed the Course of History

BILL O'NEILL

ISBN: 978-1-64845-086-0

DON'T FORGET YOUR FREE BOOKS

CONTENTS

Introduction 1

A Simple Request Pinned To A Church Door 3

Cortez And Quetzalcoatl 7

You Really Can Sail Around The World 12

Great Change In A Timeless Land 16

Who Knew A Divorce Would Have Such An Impact? 19

The Earth Actually Revolves Around The Sun! 24

Try And Try Again 27

The Real-Life Shogun 30

A Voyage To The Unknown 34

Europe's First Modern War 37

Cromwell Reigns Supreme 40

Newton And The Apple 44

Steam Once Powered The World 47

Did A Key And A Kite Harness The Power Of Electricity? 50

The Shot Heard Around The World 54

It Seemed Like A Great Place For A Prison 59

Did She Really Say, "Let Them Eat Cake"? 63

How The British Navy Established Its Supremacy 66

Napoleon Was Good, But Not That Good 70

Two Wars Fought For Drug Dealers.. 74

California Was A Backwater Before 1848.. 77

1848: A Year Of Revolution 80

A Vote For Civil War 83

Killing Lincoln Didn't Help The Southern Cause 87

The War That Changed South America Forever 90

One Germany 95

The Discovery Of Diamonds In South Africa 99

"Mr. Watson — Come Here — I Want To See You." 103

So Simple Yet So Important... 106

Remember The Maine.. 110

Reaching For The Skies... 115

Russia Was Supposed To Win That War 119

Henry Ford Knew The Model T Would Change The World 125

Can You Imagine *Not* Having Antibiotics? 129

A Wrong Turn Started A World War 132

Communist Revolution And Regicide In Russia......................... 138

The Big Crash 143

How Nonviolent Protest Was Born 146

The Historic Elections Of 1932...150

Mao's Long March 153

"A Day That Will Live In Infamy"...157

Hiroshima And Nagasaki Usher In The Atomic Age 161

A Nation Was Born And An Eternal War Began.........................164

Two Lines That Shouldn't Have Been Crossed 168

A Kid From Memphis Was Introduced To The World...............171

How The Iron Curtain Became Official 175

On The Edge Of Annihilation...178

The End Of Camelot 181

"One Small Step For Mankind"...184

How Some Nerds In A Garage Changed The World...................188

Where's Afghanistan? 192

"Mr. Gorbachev, Tear Down This Wall!" 197

No One Saw It Coming...201

What Happened When The Housing Market Bubble Popped?..204

Conclusion...207

INTRODUCTION

Many historians divide world history into "ancient," "medieval," and "modern" periods, with the modern period starting around 1500 CE and being the best documented. Many of those same historians also say that it has been the events that happened and the people who lived during the last 500 years that have defined the world we live in today. Sure, the ancient Greeks and Romans had a major influence on modern government and medieval people developed the world's most practiced religions, but the fact is our modern society and the countries we live in are the direct results of comparatively more recent events.

And make no mistake, quite a few exciting things have taken place in the last 500 years.

In *The Encyclopedia of Very Important Events through Modern History*, we take a look at 54 of the most important events since 1500 that have molded our modern world. Each of these events is examined and then their short-term and long-term effects are discussed.

We'll look at some wars - such as the Thirty Year's War, the Sengoku, and the Korean War - with an emphasis on how they impacted the people involved in them at the time and how their effects can be seen even today.

1

Specific battles, and even some moments *during* battles, are covered that had a major impact on the world.

But history isn't just about wars; this book covers any and all major events that had notable repercussions, from the discovery of antibiotics to the pivotal elections around the world in 1932, and from the Wall Street Crash of 1929 to the 9-11 Attacks and even the introduction of Elvis Presley to a national audience.

If it was an earth-shattering event that happened in the last 500 years, there's a good chance it's in this book.

But this isn't your ordinary history book. Sure, we look at the most important events of the last 500 years in chronological order, but we do so in a fun, lively way that brings history to life. So, whether you're a history buff, a bookworm, or just a lover of knowledge, I guarantee that you'll enjoy reading this book and learn a thing or two in the process.

Sit back, relax, and get ready to be amazed by the most important events in modern history.

A SIMPLE REQUEST PINNED
TO A CHURCH DOOR

Our journey through history begins on October 31, 1517, in the city of Wittenberg, Saxony, which is today part of Germany. It was on that day when a little-known Catholic monk and professor of theology named Martin Luther pinned a protest against some of the Catholic Church's practices to the door of All Saints' Church in Wittenberg, although some modern scholars believe the story of the posting on the church was added later.

Either way, Luther also sent a letter outlining his protest, which became known as the *Ninety-Five Theses*, to the Archbishop of Mainz, thereby forever sealing his fate as well as the fates of millions of people around the world. You see, Luther may not have intended to overthrow the Catholic Church or start a new church, but that's exactly what happened.

Before we get to that, let's start with some of what Luther wrote in the *Ninety-Five Theses*. Each of his major points - the theses - were areas of conflict he had with the Church. The first several theses dealt with the Church's sacrament of penance (confession to a priest), which Luther believed should be more personal. He thought that God alone could only truly absolve a person of their sins.

Then there was the idea of Church indulgences.

An indulgence is basically a form of penance for sins one has committed. During the Middle Ages, the nobles paid the Church in land and money to have their sins absolved and so that their less savory family members could make it into the pearly gates. Most people today, even Catholics, find the idea of paying for entrance into Heaven preposterous, but it was widely accepted in the Middle Ages.

You have to remember that people were far less educated back then, and the Church was generally looked at quite positively. After all, it was the king who taxed you and sent you to war, not the Church. All the Church asked for was some tithes for their coffers.

Luther also had a problem with that! He thought the peasants were paying the Church enough for the pope to live in splendor. In fact, the entire *Ninety-Five Theses* really came down to the power of the pope. Luther challenged the idea of "papal supremacy", which held that the pope was the first and last authority on any and all spiritual and biblical matters.

As soon as Luther's *Theses* were found on the church door, or his letter to the archbishop was received, or both, controversy followed. There were vigorous debates between Luther and other Church intellectuals. The Church begged and then demanded that he recant his rebellious ideas, and when he refused, Luther was excommunicated in January 1521.

Although the spiritual home that Luther knew was gone from his life, a new religious movement was forming around him. But before he could take things further, he had to stay alive!

There was talk of burning Luther at the stake, which was a common punishment for heretics in the Middle Ages. The Church ultimately deferred the prosecution of Luther to the secular authorities in the Holy Roman Empire (the Holy Roman Empire was basically medieval Germany; but as the 18th-century French philosopher Voltaire later wrote, it was "neither holy nor Roman.").

At his trial in 1521, Luther refused to recant what he wrote, leading the Diet of Worms (Assembly), which was the political/government assembly of the Holy Roman Empire, to ban his writings and put a warrant out for his arrest.

Luckily for Luther, though, the Holy Roman Empire was historically a bit of a mess. It was a collection of German-speaking kingdoms, duchies, and counties that would agree to work together and send a representative to elect an emperor who had nominal rule over all of them. Ambitious nobles who used the inherent weakness of the system to their advantage were quite common and when Luther became an outlaw in 1521, Frederick III, the Elector of Saxony, hid the rebel theologian in his Wartburg Castle for about a year.

This is where the great impacts of Luther's *Ninety-Five Theses* began to be realized.

Luther used his time in exile to translate the New Testament from Greek into German. Translating the New Testament in one year is a feat in itself, but the fact that he did so in a language other than Latin was revolutionary. The New Testament was originally written in Greek and later translated into Latin, Coptic, and Syriac, but never into the common European languages.

The Church leaders of the Middle Ages believed that the Bible was only to be read by the priests and the other members of the hierarchy. The rest of the flock would get all of their information from the priests.

Besides, most people couldn't read at the time anyway! But by translating the Bible into German, Luther inadvertently helped millions of his countrymen, and later Europeans generally, become literate. Reading was acceptable if it was done for religious purposes.

The true impact of Luther's *Ninety-Five Theses*, though, was that it proved to be the start of the Reformation. Luther evaded arrest and execution and lived out his life to what was at the time the relatively advanced age of 62, but not before he founded the religious movement known as Protestantism and the particular religion/sect of Lutheranism.

Today, Lutheranism is the primary Christian religion in Scandinavia and parts of Germany, while Protestants combine to make up 37% of all Christians worldwide.

Keep reading to see how Luther's ideas continued to impact the course of history in the 1500s and 1660s to the point where more than a few people lost their heads, literally.

CORTEZ AND QUETZALCOATL

Before we get to how Luther's ideas created a ripple effect of important events, let's take a detour from Europe to the New World.

The New World was what Europeans called the Americas in the 1500s because it had only recently been discovered by Europeans. You probably know that in 1492 Columbus "sailed the ocean blue" and discovered the New World, and although that was certainly an important event, it was just before the timeline of our book.

So, let's take a look at the next big event that happened in the New World.

In 1519, the Aztecs were the dominant people in the Central Mexican Valley, which was an area that is more or less equivalent to modern-day Mexico City. The Aztecs continued the temple-building tradition of their predecessors in the region, constructing great pyramids where they gave sacrifices to their gods, usually in the form of live humans.

Yes, as impressive as Aztec culture was, it was also a bit brutal, which was the result of the Aztecs worshipping several fairly brutal gods.

There was the war god, Huitzilopochtli, who particularly loved alive and beating human hearts. Then there was the god of fertility and rain, Tlaloc, who also had a thing for blood. And at the end of this bloody pantheon was the feathered serpent god, Quetzalcoatl (the god of the Morning Star).

The Aztecs developed many myths about Quetzalcoatl and their other gods and goddesses, but almost all of them were passed down through the generations orally and those that were eventually put into writing were only done so just before or after the fall of the Aztec Empire at the hands of the Spanish. But according to one myth, Quetzalcoatl created humanity from a primeval chaotic void and then consumed himself in flames. It was believed that he would one day return as a white cloud to save humanity from itself.

Enter Hernan Cortes. (Hernán Cortés de Monroy y Pizarro Altamirano)

Hernan Cortes was born in 1485 in the Spanish Kingdom of Castile to the lower nobility. It was a time of great transition and violence in Spain and the Iberian Peninsula. The Spanish Christians were in the final stages of expelling the Muslims from the peninsula in what became known as the *Reconquista*. Meanwhile, several Portuguese explorers were making important discoveries, most notably Vasco da Gama's circumnavigation of Africa in 1497-99 and subsequent return to Lisbon. And of course, there was the Italian Christopher Columbus' New World discovery in 1492.

So, with all this going on, Cortes made his way to what would later become Cuba, where he planned his mission that would change history.

Cortes was an ambitious, greedy, and relatively violent young man, which were all traits that proved to be useful in the New World in the early 1500s. After hearing about "cities of gold" and such in what is today Mexico, Cortes organized an expedition to explore the mysterious land. As alcalde/mayor of Santiago, Cuba, Cortes had the resources to put an expedition together, but he was denied a permit at the last minute.

But men like Cortes don't need no stinking permit, so he decided to lead the expedition anyway!

After first making contact with Spaniards on the Yucatan Peninsula, and picking up some Indian translators, Cortes and his men sailed north to what is now Veracruz, Mexico, where they landed sometime in April, 1519.

Cortes then had the ships destroyed, thereby making the mission do or die for him and his 500 men. They were equipped with 16 horses, muskets, crossbows, and a couple of cannons, which they would need in their conflicts with the Aztecs.

Cortes soon found out, though, that the Aztecs were not very popular with the other indigenous peoples of Mexico. The Aztecs often raided the other cities and peoples of the region to use in their human sacrifice rituals. No wonder they weren't very popular! So, the clever Cortes used this to his advantage by gaining a considerable number of Indian allies in Veracruz.

Then when Cortes finally met the Aztec Emperor Montezuma II, the Quetzalcoatl myth came into play.

It's important to know that when the Spanish met the Aztecs, it was a classic "first contact" scenario, and the Spanish had the advantage. The Aztecs had never seen Europeans before, so their fair skin and different colored eyes and hair made them seem as though they were from another world. The Aztecs had also never seen horses, metal armor, crossbows, muskets, or cannons either, so everything combined made many of them believe that the Spanish really were gods.

It's impossible to know for sure whether Montezuma believed Cortes was the earthly avatar of Quetzalcoatl, but he did invite him and his men to the Aztec capital city of Tenochtitlan, which proved to be a fatal mistake.

Cortes and the Spanish made Montezuma a prisoner, and when the Aztecs finally realized the Spanish were no gods and expelled them from their city, it was too late. Cortes returned with more Indian allies, laid siege to Tenochtitlan, and levelled it to the ground on August 13, 1521.

The impacts of Cortes' initial landing in Veracruz in 1519 and his conquest of the Aztecs in 1521 could fill several books, but we'll try to relate a few of the most pivotal ones here.

The first is the destruction of the greatest of all Pre-Columbian empires. The Aztecs were the military and cultural force that influenced all of central America at the time, but when Cortes and his merry band of conquistadors showed up, all that changed. The Spanish immediately became the top people on the totem pole and their control was extended from the Rio Grande all the way to Tierra del Fuego.

The Spanish Empire would go on to become *the* world empire of the 1500s thanks in large part to Cortes' conquest of Mexico. Cortes' conquest also ensured that most of the Americas south of the Rio Grande would be Spanish speaking and Roman Catholic, which in many ways is even more important.

Although the Spanish Empire eventually collapsed, the cultural legacy of Cortes' conquest can be heard in the speech of most Latin Americans and seen in their churches from Mexico City to Buenos Aires.

YOU REALLY CAN SAIL
AROUND THE WORLD

You probably get the idea by now that modern history began with a bang in the early 1500s. It was like a cork was taken out of the bottle that was the Middle Ages, and all kinds of ideas and inspirations began to flow. Now, don't get me wrong. Many people died (we've covered that a bit and will get to some more later), but the truth is that there was a new spirit of optimism in the world, especially in Western Europe.

Some Europeans were driven by a desire to question the old monarchal and religious orders. Others were grasped by a love of riches. Others still were enthralled with a sense of adventure.

One person who kind of embodied all of those traits was Portuguese explorer Ferdinand Magellan. Similar to Cortes, Magellan belonged to a lower noble family. Born in Portugal in 1480, from a young age he showed plenty of ambition and promise.

Portugal was in a similar position to Spain at the time and its people were exploring and conquering locations in Africa and India. The Portuguese eventually monopolized the route around Africa to India. Magellan took part in many early expeditions and even played a role in the Portuguese conquest of the Spice Islands in 1511, which are today part of Indonesia.

But the Spice Islands were a long way from Portugal, so Magellan began thinking of an easier way to get there.

Contrary to common belief, most *educated* Europeans didn't think the world was flat when Columbus made his famous voyage in 1492. The ancient Greeks actually first theorized that the Earth was a sphere, and in the 2nd century CE Greek geographer, Ptolemy, put that idea into maps, although those maps were lost to most people until the 1400s when copies reemerged and were circulated throughout Europe.

And when the New World was discovered, it was proven that the world was a sphere.

But even the most seasoned navigators didn't know how *big* the Earth was or how large the Pacific Ocean was. Most people thought the Earth was just too large to circumnavigate with the technology of the period and that the Pacific was basically a vast watery desert.

Yet any true explorer worth his salt in the 1500s would jump at the chance of attempting the feat, so Magellan went to King Manuel I of Portugal with his plan to lead an expedition to the Spice Islands via the New World. Unfortunately for Magellan, the king wasn't as forward-thinking as him and, like most people, thought any such expedition was doomed to fail.

So, Magellan did the almost unthinkable and brought his plan to the Spanish King Charles I, who would be the future Charles V, Holy Roman Emperor. This was a pretty big deal because Portugal and Spain were *the* major superpowers at the time. It would be like an American astronaut going to work for the Soviet space agency during the Cold War!

Whether Charles I thought Magellan could succeed, or if he funded Magellan to spite the Portuguese or a combination of both, is a subject of historical debate. Regardless, after getting funded by the Spanish crown, Magellan and about 270 men left Spain on five ships on September 20, 1519.

The voyage was difficult, to say the least.

Magellan and his men had to avoid pirates and angry Portuguese naval ships. They also dealt with disease, hunger, thirst, the elements, and attempted mutinies. And that was all before they even passed through the dangerous tip of South America and what would become known as the Strait of Magellan.

When the force arrived in what is today the Philippines on March 16, 1521, they had successfully crossed the Pacific and were on their way home. After getting supplies, Magellan decided to convert the locals to Christianity and found some success as well as resistance.

Magellan was killed on April 27, 1521, by natives who weren't quite ready to take up the cross. But the show must go on, right? Navigator Juan Sebastian Elcano led the expedition the rest of the way back to Spain, finally arriving there on September 6, 1522, with only one ship and 18 or 19 men.

Despite the extreme loss of life and the fact that the organizer and original leader of the expedition didn't live to see it completed, Magellan's expedition was a major success and considered one of the biggest turning points in modern world history.

To understand the magnitude of what Magellan and Elcano did, the closest achievement I can think of is the first men who walked on the Moon. The Magellan expedition truly went into uncharted territory and as a result, forwarded humanity's scientific knowledge in several categories, including cartography, geography, geology, biology, and anthropology.

Magellan's expedition also spawned other attempts that were eventually more and more successful, such as Francis Drake's expedition, thereby making the world a little bit smaller, so to speak.

Finally, the expedition helped cement Spain's place at the top of the geopolitical pecking order for about 100 years. Spain claimed all the lands Magellan and his crew "discovered," which included the Philippines and other islands in the south Pacific.

You could say Magellan made one "giant leap for mankind" — hundreds of years before that phrase was uttered!

GREAT CHANGE IN
A TIMELESS LAND

Not long after Martin Luther began his religious revolution in 1517, great religious and cultural changes came to India in 1526 when an Islamic group known as the Mughals conquered most of the land and established a dynasty. To understand the significance of the Mughal conquest, it's important to take a look at what was happening in India before the Mughals arrived.

For most of its history, India wasn't one country as it is today but was a collection of kingdoms and principalities that were divided by the dozens of different languages that the people spoke and the many different ethnic groups from which the people came. India was also a land of many different religions: Hinduism, Buddhism, and Jainism were all born in India.

And despite some of the great innovations that came out of India throughout the centuries - the concept of zero and some interesting anatomical observations, just to name two - ancient and medieval India has often been viewed as a place where time stood still.

India was a place where gurus, philosophers, and yogis practiced their craft without a thought to time or place. In fact, time was - for the most part - irrelevant to these people. Well, that's not exactly the case, but it really seemed like that to the world outside of India for most of history.

India did have contacts with the outside world, primarily to the east via Buddhism, but also sporadically with the west through trade and warfare.

This all changed in an instant when a guy named Babur (a descendant of Genghis and Timur Khan) led an Islamic army into India in 1526, quickly conquering northern India, with his successors eventually taking all but the southernmost tip of the subcontinent. It also included most of the area of what are today the modern countries of Afghanistan and Bangladesh.

It was a pretty impressive feat for the man who was descended from Genghis Khan, which is why they were called the Mughals (Mongols). However, the military conquest isn't the most important part of this event; it's everything that happened after.

Babur and the Mughal's conquest of India proved to be one of the most important events in modern history for several reasons, some of which are still felt today.

First, the Mughals were able to win the war largely due to their use of gunpowder weapons. Gunpowder had been around for hundreds of years at that point, but Europeans had only fairly recently invented muskets and cannons that allowed the invention to be used in newer, deadlier ways. The Mughals acquired gunpowder weapons from the Ottoman Turks and then used those weapons against the Indians.

From India, cannons and muskets then made their way east where they were eventually utilized in the lands where gunpowder was first invented hundreds of years earlier, completing a circle of the invention.

Funny how history works sometimes!

The second major impact of the Mughal conquest of India was much more profound and long-lasting. The Mughals brought Islam with them during their conquest, and although there were some Muslims in India before 1526, their numbers increased dramatically after that time. The entire northwestern portion of India (what is today Pakistan) became predominantly Muslim, influencing old religious ideas in the region as well as new ones, such as Sikhism.

The Mughals also left a very visible imprint on the world's second-most populous country.

Today, India's most recognized monument, the Taj Mahal, is a testament to its Mughal history. The Taj Mahal was built from 1632 to 1653 as a mausoleum for the Mughal Emperor Shah Jahan's favorite wife (he had four).

The Mughal conquest also brought religious conflicts to India that have sporadically erupted from time to time, shaking the seemingly timeless country out of its isolation.A Many of these issues remain unresolved, although at least one man we'll look at later made a valiant attempt to solve some of them.

WHO KNEW A DIVORCE WOULD HAVE SUCH AN IMPACT?

Today, divorce is an unfortunate (or in some cases, fortunate) part of our modern world. Around half of all marriages end in divorce for a variety of reasons, ranging from infidelity to money problems, and usually a combination of reasons. There's a good chance you've either been divorced or grew up in a divorced family.

But things weren't always this way.

For most of human history, the saying "till death do us part" was more or less true.

This was especially so in medieval Europe, where divorce was not allowed by the Roman Catholic Church or even the Orthodox Churches in Eastern Europe, for that matter. And this was the case for the nobles as well as the peasants. To the Church, marriage was a holy sacrament that couldn't be broken.

Noble men did have the means to have mistresses and although this wasn't supported by the Church, leaders often turned a blind eye.

But divorce was strictly forbidden and wasn't even considered, at least until the Reformation started taking place. As new churches began forming in Europe, the idea of marriage and divorce was questioned, quietly, until 1534 when it played a central role in part of the Reformation.

Henry VIII is not remembered as one of England's greatest kings, but there's no doubt he was one of the most memorable ones. Born in 1491 to the royal Tudor family, just as the world was changing, young Henry was raised in the world of the Renaissance and the early Reformation.

Although Henry did display some early intellectual curiosity, his primary interest in life was chasing women. Yes, Henry was a bit of a playboy. When he wasn't attending to affairs of the state, he was partying, eating good food, hunting game, and pursuing ladies.

And the ladies liked Henry. Well, they kind of *had* to like him. He was the king, after all, and he was known as a man who wouldn't take no for an answer. Henry is best known for his six marriages and poor ability to keep them together. He had wives two and five—Anne Boleyn and Catherine Howard—beheaded for reasons that may or may not have been true and, in any case, were actions (infidelity, for instance) that would not be executable offenses in most places today.

Wife three, Jane Seymour, died while they were married; he had his marriage to wife four, Anne of Cleves, annulled; and wife six, Catherine Parr, outlived him.

But it was his marriage to his first wife, Catherine of Aragon, that led to the important historical events of 1534.

Henry and Catherine were wed in 1509 as a marriage of convenience, to say the least. Catherine was actually married to Henry's older brother, Arthur, but when he died in 1502 Henry inherited the future crown and his brother's wife. Since Catherine was previously married, the Church needed to give special dispensation to the new marriage.

Needless to say, it wasn't a marriage full of love, lust, or much of anything else.

The marriage was clearly done to gain an ally in Spain (remember they were *the* power in the early 1500s) and to give Henry a male heir. The results of the first reason were mixed at best and in terms of the second, Catherine was only able to give birth to a live daughter, Mary.

So, Henry began looking elsewhere for love, affection, and a potential male heir, but he faced one major obstacle - the Church.

Henry was actually a devout Catholic, although not necessarily a moral person. That may seem like a strange thing but remember back to the idea of indulgences - guys like Henry loved the fact that they could buy their way into Heaven! So, to remain a good Catholic and move on with his life to marry his mistress, Anne Boleyn, who he hoped would give him a male heir, he needed an annulment.

An annulment, of course, is like a divorce, but it's the Church's way of saying the marriage never happened. Annulments were only given under special circumstances back then, including non-consummation of the marriage. But Henry and Catherine and obviously consummated their marriage and the pope was particularly close to the Spanish royal family, who opposed the annulment. Henry arranged to receive the annulment in 1533 which was not officially recognized by the Catholic Church.

So, although Henry was officially denied, he went ahead with his marriage to Anne Boleyn anyway and in 1534 declared himself the Supreme Head of the English Church. The pope reacted by excommunicating Henry from the Catholic Church, thereby giving birth to the Church of England.

The impact of Henry's divorce from Catherine was monumental. The Church of England's formation helped the Reformation to gain steam. From 1536 to 1540, Henry dissolved the Catholic monasteries in England, taking all their wealth and setting off a massive round of anti-Catholic violence.

But Henry was still at heart a Catholic, so when hardcore Protestants in his inner circle became upset that the Church of England was little more than an English Catholic Church that allowed divorce, they began speaking out.

In response, Henry had a bunch of Protestants arrested and burned at the stake.

One day, Catholics were burned and the next it was Protestants, and then Catholics again. I guess you could say Henry was an equal opportunity stake burner!

Things settled down a bit by the end of Henry's reign, but after he died, the religious conflict started again when his daughter with Catherine of Aragon, Mary, came to the throne and initiated anti-Protestant measures.

Religious warfare became a regular thing in England well into the 1600s (we'll get to some of that a bit later), and the British Isles are still religiously divided to a certain extent: Catholic Ireland, Protestant England, and a divided Scotland.

As for divorce? Well, it took a while for divorce to catch on, I guess you could say. The Church of England began giving annulments more freely, especially to the upper class, but no-fault divorce didn't become a reality in England and most Western countries until the late 1960s and 1970s.

With that said, good or bad, divorce, as we know it today, wouldn't have been possible without the influence of Henry VIII.

THE EARTH ACTUALLY REVOLVES AROUND THE SUN!

I mentioned previously how the 2nd century CE Greek geographer Ptolemy argued, correctly, that the world was a sphere. He did that by adding longitudinal and latitudinal lines on the map. Ptolemy also wrote about astrology, astronomy, and other sciences, which prove that he was one of the greatest minds of late antiquity.

But not *everything* he said was true.

One of Ptolemy's big intellectual fails was the geocentric model of the universe, which held that the Earth was the center of the solar system (and also the entire universe). Despite all the great ideas the Greeks came up with, this was perhaps their biggest failure, and it went unchecked for centuries.

People everywhere just took it as a matter of fact that the Earth was the center of it all.

It makes sense when you think about it. There's no real evidence that any of the other planets are inhabited, so why would people in the Middle Ages think that the Earth *wasn't* the center of it all?

But as all the new ideas of the Renaissance, Reformation, and Age of Exploration we've already discussed were being bandied around, a few brave souls began questioning the "science" of the time.

These people were as brave as Luther or Magellan because their ideas were contrary to the teaching of the secular governments *and* the Church. In other words, those promoting rebellious ideas could've found themselves turned into tinder for a barbeque!

Perhaps the most influential of all these rebellious scientists of the 1500s was a Polish, or German (his ethnicity/nationality depends upon who you ask), polymath named Nicolaus Copernicus. Born in 1473 in Prussia to a wealthy commoner family, Copernicus was quite precocious from an early age, learning Latin, Greek, and Italian in addition to his native languages of German and Polish.

Copernicus would go on to earn several degrees in the hard sciences, humanities, and church law, making him the epitome of a "Renaissance man."

But as impressive as Copernicus' background was, it was his Earth-shattering (yes, pun intended) idea of heliocentrism or the basic idea that the Sun is at the center of the solar system, that defined him.

Copernicus began contemplating the idea of heliocentrism in the early 1500s as he worked as a professional scholar. In 1543, he published his theory - as it was at the time, anyway - in his book, *De revolutionibus orbium coelestium* (*On the Revolutions of the Heavenly Spheres*).

The impact of the book's publication was profound on so many levels and is considered by some to be the greatest scientific discovery of the modern era, and quite possibly of all history.

First, the heliocentric theory challenged all the old scientific, political, and social orders in just about every way. Even the

Church, which held fast to the geocentric model of the universe, saw the heliocentric model as a threat. Copernicus may have suffered some serious repercussions from the Church, but he died in 1543 at the age of 70, just after his book was published.

The most profound impact Copernicus' heliocentric model of the universe had was the way the world was seen. No longer did people think of the Earth as the center of the universe, becoming aware that even if humans are alone in the universe, it doesn't revolve around humans, literally and figuratively.

When Copernicus' heliocentric model was accepted as a scientific fact and not just another theory, it opened the door for a plethora of new scientists to test their theories and make even greater advances, some of which we'll get to later in our book.

It's difficult to think what the world would be like if we still went by the geocentric model. Maybe someone else would've come up with the heliocentric model of the universe, but there's no telling how far behind we'd be in terms of technological advances if Copernicus hadn't made his thinking known.

TRY AND TRY AGAIN

By the late 1500s, the Spanish and the Portuguese were making sturdy progress colonizing the New World, and in the case of the Spanish, they were literally bringing boatloads of gold and silver back to Europe. The effects of that would later cripple Spain through inflation, but in the meantime, it served to make them the premier world power.

But the British had plans to catch up.

As early explorers were mapping out the coastline of what would later become the United States, in 1578 Britain's Queen Elizabeth decided she would fund expeditions to explore and colonize the New World. Since the Spanish and Portuguese had most lands south of the Rio Grande, the British became involved in a race against the Dutch and French to colonize North America.

Sir Walter Raleigh, the namesake of Raleigh, North Carolina, organized the first British expedition to what would become Roanoke Island in 1584, deciding that the sea-battered location would make a great place to start a colony.

Raleigh may have been brave and an excellent navigator, but his city planning skills were a bit lacking. Still, there were more about 108 British citizens who were willing to make a go of colonizing Roanoke under the leadership of Ralph Lane in 1585.

Raleigh would wisely sit the expedition out.

The colony was ill-equipped for the long-term and was not in a very good location for farming. To make matters worse, the goodwill they originally cultivated with the local Indian tribes had evaporated by the spring of 1586, turning Roanoke into an armed camp.

It was more than the colonists had bargained for, so they returned to England in the summer.

Raleigh, though, had an official charter to colonize the New World, so he organized another expedition and found 112 to 121 volunteers—men, women, and children—who were willing to give it a go in the New World under the leadership of John White in 1587.

Raleigh knew that the British had burned too many bridges on Roanoke Island, so he ordered the expedition to go north to the Chesapeake Bay. But as we've seen already in this book - and as we'll see numerous other times in the coming chapters—many of the biggest events in history are unplanned.

The colonists were ordered off the ships by the sailors at Roanoke on July 22, so they were forced to meet their destiny on what would be the island of doom.

The colonists found things eerily calm on Roanoke, with the houses intact, although overgrown with vegetation.

Things could have gone several different ways at this point. According to White, the colonists attempted to learn from the mistakes of their predecessors by smoothing things over with the Indian tribes. However, in their attempts to do so, they made enemies of the Croatans, who were the only Indians they were on good terms with.

Roanoke once again became an armed camp, and the colonists knew they wouldn't survive without some reinforcements. Consequently, White was sent back to England on August 27 for help.

War with Spain kept White from returning to Roanoke until April 18, 1590. None of the colonists was found, most of the houses had been dismantled, and everything of value, including small boats, were gone. White did find the word CROATAN inscribed on the palisade wall of the settlement, which he took to mean that the colonists had relocated to Croatan Island a short distance away.

Expeditions were later sent to find the lost colonists, but none were ever found.

The disappearance of the Roanoke Colony represents a major turning point in world history. The British, who were at number three or maybe even four in the race for empire during the era, could've just called everything off after the two disasters at Roanoke but instead, they tried and tried again.

The result was better funded and equipped British expeditions of North America that were successful in large part because the explorers and colonists learned from the mistakes of Roanoke. Future British expeditions in North America were much more heavily armed, but they also used a fair amount of diplomacy when dealing with the natives.

Finally, if Roanoke hadn't failed, Jamestown may never have been established in 1607. Jamestown became the British's first successful permanent colony in North America and was for decades the center of early American culture.

Jamestown also became a pretty cool living history museum centuries later!

THE REAL-LIFE SHOGUN

James Clavell's 1975 novel, *Shogun*, became a best seller because it had something for everyone: adventure, romance, action, and exotic locations. The novel was so popular it was translated into several languages and inspired a nine-hour 1980 miniseries of the same name. The story follows a British sailor who is shipwrecked in Japan in the late 1500s, suffering many trials and tribulations in the process.

But as fun as *Shogun* the novel and miniseries may be, it was based on one very important event that changed Japanese and world history - the *Sengoku*.

Sengoku is a Japanese word that roughly translates as "era or period of warring states." It refers to the period from 1467 when the Japanese nobility fought for control over the archipelago nation until 1603 when the Tokugawa Shogunate was established. You see, before that time, Japan was rarely unified under the emperor and when it was, the emperor was usually no more than a figurehead.

The true power was held by the shoguns, who were powerful warlords or generals. These men were appointed by the emperors to rule during times of peace and when Japan was more or less unified, such as during the Kamakura Shogunate from 1185 to 1333.

Under the shoguns were the daimyo, who were regional lords. And fighting for the shoguns and daimyos were the samurai. If you're reading this and think the medieval Japanese system resembles the medieval European system, you're right and it might be easier to think of it that way.

The emperor was similar to the pope and below him, the shogun was like a king, while the daimyos were like the many dukes, barons, and counts found throughout medieval Europe. And the samurai were basically medieval Japanese knights.

The system worked well for a couple of reasons. The first was that the shogunates, which were dynasties similar to European royal families, often did well in uniting Japan. The shoguns would rally the daimyos and samurai against common outside foes, such as the Mongols while making sure none of the other shoguns became too powerful.

But by the late 1400s, the Ashikaga Shogunate grew weak and in the 1500s the Sengoku was raging across the land.

And then the second factor in Japan's long political stability and success came into play.

As you probably know, Japan is an island nation. Well, to be specific, it's an archipelago comprised of several hundred islands, which made foreign invasion in the ancient and medieval periods almost impossible. The Mongols tried it in the 1200s, but they were defeated by an army of samurai.

That's not to say that Japan's geography kept ideas from entering the land. Japan inherited its writing system from China, as well as Buddhism and Confucianism. And when the first Europeans began arriving there in the mid-1500s, they brought with them gunpowder weapons.

Remember the circuitous route of gunpowder weapons I mentioned earlier with the Mughals?

Well, when gunpowder weapons made their way back to the Far East, they had their biggest and most immediate impact in Japan.

As the daimyos knocked each other off throughout the 1500s, none gained an upper hand until Tokugawa Ieyasu stepped up and made some clever moves. First, he unified the clans and daimyos of eastern Japan under his leadership, then he led an army of nearly 90,000 men against an army of western clans led by Ishida Mitsunari of just under the same size.

The two armies met at a place called Sekigahara in central Japan on October 21, 1600. Although the Western Army had a strategic advantage based on their defensive position, Tokugawa brought a regiment of arquebuses (early muskets) with him.

The battle was tough, but the tide turned when Tokugawa ordered his men to fire their arquebuses on the forces of a daimyo who was trying to play neutral. After the shots, the daimyo joined Tokugawa and the battle was won.

Resistance continued until 1603 when Tokugawa unified Japan under his rule and began the Tokugawa Shogunate, which lasted until 1868.

The historical implications of the Sengoku in general and the Battle of Sekigahara, in particular, were immediate, as the Japanese took a hard line against foreign influence. Foreigners were rarely allowed into the Land of the Rising Sun and Western ideas, such as Christianity, were officially suppressed. Japan then became somewhat of a mystery to the rest of the world until it reopened in 1868.

Once Japan did open to the world in 1868, it went the other way, so to speak, outlawing many traditional ways and soaking up as many Western ideas as it could, as quickly as it could.

It's difficult to say how Japan would have developed if another shogun had won the Sengoku and then decided to continue Japan's openness to the West. Maybe all or parts of it would have been conquered and colonized, as happened in China?

Maybe World War II wouldn't have happened in the Pacific?

It's difficult to say, but we do know that the Sengoku and Tokugawa's victory in it decided the fate of Japan for several hundred years.

A VOYAGE TO THE UNKNOWN

One of the most defining events in American history actually happened long before the United States was even a country, and it took place on a ship in the Atlantic Ocean. As we'll see in our next story, the year 1620 was quite busy - "happening," so to speak, throughout Europe.

Most of Europe was involved in a bloody religious war in the Holy Roman Empire, but England managed to stay out of that one. England's king, James I, was ruler over England, Wales, Scotland, and Ireland, so he had enough of his own religious problems to deal with. Catholics continued to be the vast majority in Ireland and were still quite numerous in northern England and Scotland. Scotland also became a hotbed of Calvinist activity.

Calvinists were Protestants who followed the teachings or were influenced by, 16th-century French reformer John Calvin. Calvinist beliefs were many and ranged from church to church, but most believed in the idea of "predestination" and also followed the Bible quite literally.

The Calvinists in Scotland and England became known as Puritans because they wanted to purify the Church of England, which they thought was too Catholic.

Well, they were more or less correct with that belief because if you remember, Henry VIII's true motivation to break away from the Catholic Church was to get rid of his first wife and then his other wives.

So, eventually many Puritans tried to change the Church of England while others saw it as too evil to save and decided to separate completely from it. The separatists became known as the Pilgrims. Separating and forming their own churches wasn't a legal option, though. The Pilgrims faced heavy fines for not attending church and their leaders also faced imprisonment, or worse.

So, with their big hats and big belt buckles (which were actually in style in the early 1600s), and those big guns, the Pilgrims left England first for Holland and then back to England before making their final and permanent move to North America. The Pilgrims were granted land and sailed for what they thought would be Virginia in two ships, the *Mayflower* and *Speedwell*.

The *Speedwell* repeatedly took on water, so it had to turn back to England and transfer its passengers and what it could of its supplies to the *Mayflower*.

When the Pilgrims finally arrived off the shore of North America on November 9, 1620, just over two months later, the approximate 102 passengers and 50 crew members on the *Mayflower* (one had been added during the trip with a birth) were ready to put their feet on solid ground. The problem was that they were off the coast of Cape Cod, Massachusetts, which was a long way from Virginia.

The Pilgrims' leader, William Bradford, knew that this would be tough, especially since the non-Pilgrim men among them, whom they called "strangers," wanted to head south to Virginia. You see, although Bradford and some of the other Pilgrims may not have particularly liked the idea of non-Pilgrims among them, their skills would be needed since most of the Pilgrims were farmers.

So, on November 21, Bradford presented a short document of just under 200 words for all the men on the *Mayflower*, Pilgrim and stranger, to sign. The document, which became known as the *Mayflower Compact*, gave every man who signed it, and in what would become the Plymouth Colony once they went ashore, an equal vote and rights among his peers.

The *Mayflower Compact* proved to be historically significant because it was the first official declaration of political and human rights in the New World, and it established the idea of majority rule in what would become the United States.

As much as the *Mayflower's* voyage was a trip into the unknown, physically, it was also a journey into uncharted political, social, and cultural waters. When the men of the *Mayflower* signed the *Mayflower Compact,* they left a legacy that would prove to be the political and civic inspiration for the later United States, but also for every government on the globe that claims to be democratic, whether they realize it or not.

EUROPE'S FIRST MODERN WAR

As we take our trip through modern history's most important events and move into the 1600s, you should see by this point that one monumental event often has a cascading effect that creates even more major events later.

It's difficult to say for sure what Martin Luther thought would happen when he nailed his complaints to that church door in 1517. He likely thought something would happen otherwise he wouldn't have done it, but he probably didn't think it would unleash nearly 200 years of sectarian violence across Europe!

Since the Holy Roman Empire was ground zero of the Reformation, and because its many small kingdoms were autonomous, warfare broke out in the mid-1500s between the Catholics and Protestants. The two groups eventually saw those outside forces, such as the Ottoman Turks, who weren't even Christians, were a threat to both sides. Consequently, they signed the Peace of Augsburg in 1555, which allowed each kingdom within the empire to choose whether to be Catholic or Lutheran.

No other faith, even other Christian sects, were allowed.

An uneasy peace lasted for more than half a century, although Protestantism continued to grow among the nobles and commoners. Then the uneasy peace ended when Protestants in Bohemia rebelled against its Catholic king, Ferdinand II in 1618. The Protestants started things off by throwing two of Ferdinand's representatives from the wall of a castle.

Not exactly diplomatic!

So, the Thirty Years' War began in earnest in 1614, with the Protestant German-speaking kingdoms lined up on one side and the Catholic kingdoms on the other. Later, other kingdoms, such as the Netherlands, Denmark, and France became involved, with Catholic France siding with the Protestants, demonstrating that the Thirty Years' War was not entirely about religion.

Ferdinand II reluctantly became the Holy Roman Emperor in 1619, and despite being an uber Catholic, he tried to end the war in 1629 with the *Edict of Restitution*. The edict stated that the original religious affiliations of the kingdoms in the empire at the Peace of Augsburg would be reaffirmed. That sounds fair, right?

Wrong, at least to the Protestants. In the time since the Peace of Augsburg, Protestantism had grown, so when the edict was declared, Protestants lost plenty of titles, lands, etc.

So, the Thirty Years' War went on and on and on…, until the smoke of the war finally cleared in 1648.

When the war was over, it was clear that Europe had been forever changed. For starters, up to eight million people died in the war, making it the deadliest war in history until that time. The Thirty Years' War also affected other wars and military conflicts in Europe during the 1600s - the continent was a real killing zone during that era!

The Thirty Years' War was also one of the first truly "modern" wars, not just in Europe but in the entire world. The armies on both sides used muskets, cannons, and long pikes instead of swords and heavy armor.

The armies were also smaller and more specialized, which is still the norm today. Mercenaries played a major role in the war, often switching sides and subjecting the civilian population to numerous cruelties.

Civilians have always been victims in wars, but civilian atrocities became more widespread and pronounced during the Thirty Years' War. In better news, while the civilian population of the Holy Roman Empire suffered, a very German food staple became common.

Potatoes are a major component in German cuisine, but the South American tuber wasn't introduced to the Holy Roman Empire until the Thirty Years' War was raging through the land. Later, according to legend, King Frederick II of Prussia introduced potatoes to his army officially and it didn't take long for them to catch on. They were the perfect wartime food: cheap, filling, and since they grow *in* the ground, their fields were difficult for marauding armies to destroy.

So, out of all the misery that the Thirty Years' War brought to Europe, at least we got German potato salad out of it!

CROMWELL REIGNS SUPREME

King James may have kept England out of the Thirty Years' War, but in the 1600s, political and religious strife was never far away. Add to that the fact that muskets and cannons were relatively new toys for eager generals, mercenaries, and adventurers, it was only a matter of time before a large-scale war came to England.

We've already seen that England had some religious tensions brewing underneath the surface, and when that was mixed with political problems, it all came rushing to the surface of society in 1642 in the form of the English Civil War. The English Civil War was actually three separate conflicts, with the first taking place from 1642 to 1648, the second from 1648 to 1649, and the third from 1649 to 1651. There was still conflict up till 1653.

The English Civil War pitted the English Parliament, known as the Roundheads for their short, cropped haircuts, on one side, against the Cavaliers, who were led first by King Charles I until he got the axe in 1649, literally, and then his son, Charles II.

Other factions became involved as well, including Irish Catholics, who supported the Cavaliers, and the Scottish Covenanters, who supported both sides at various times.

Since the focus of this book is on important events, we'll focus on the most important event in the English Civil War, its ending, and how Oliver Cromwell came to power, forever changing the government in England and leaving long-lasting scars in the process.

The English Civil War began due to many issues that Charles I should've seen coming. Scotland had become part of the English crown during James I's rule (he was part of the royal line of both countries and was James VI in Scotland) and with it there were plenty of differences, especially religious. The English wanted the Scottish Church to be more in line with the Church of England, but the Scottish weren't willing to accept complete English rule.

The Parliament had also been growing in power in the previous two centuries as more and more commoners were allowed to participate. Now, it should be pointed out that these "commoners" were usually wealthy and influential men in their towns and counties, very few people still had the right to vote, and absolutely no women could vote or hold office.

Still, Parliament had by 1642 gained quite a bit of power and had become a legitimate institution in England.

So, they didn't appreciate it when the king kept dissolving their assemblies and telling them they weren't needed. The Parliament ordered Charles I to give them more power, he said no, and then the country devolved into civil war.

Things got pretty bad in England, just as bad as they were in the Holy Roman Empire around the same time. Both sides committed atrocities against the civilian population and for a while, it seemed as though no side could win.

But then a wealthy commoner named Oliver Cromwell took the reins of the Parliamentarian forces. The militarily inexperienced Cromwell quickly proved his bravery on the battlefield and later his keen insight into tactics. He fought on horseback and was promoted to commander of the Roundhead cavalry due to the bravery and skills he exhibited at the Battle of Marston Moor on July 2, 1644.

Although Cromwell had no military experience before the war, he refashioned the Parliamentarian force into a modern, professional army that became known as the New Model Army.

After Charles was captured in 1648 and beheaded in 1649, the war took on a much more brutal tone (as if it wasn't brutal enough already!), when fighting spread to Ireland.

As some loyalists and Cavaliers fled to the Emerald Isle, Cromwell followed with his army, conquering the island and massacring thousands of civilians in the process.

But Cromwell wasn't yet done. He continued to fight in the English Civil Wars and eventually became the primary victor in 1653 when Parliament made him the "Lord Protector of the Commonwealth of England, Scotland, and Ireland." The term "protector" may have given the title an air of legitimacy but for all intents and purpose, Cromwell was the modern world's first true dictator.

He only ruled for about five years before dying of a fever at the age of 59 in 1658, but the impact his rise to power had on the British Isles was immense.

First, he ensured that Britain would forever have a strong Parliament, even if a dictator ruled over them briefly.

Next, Cromwell is the major reason why so much enmity exists between the Irish and English. Thanks to Cromwell, the Irish were ruled by the English for more than 300 years and the atrocities they suffered under him were repeated several times over the centuries.

Finally, Scotland's brand of Christianity flourished because of Cromwell. As the fighting grew more intense throughout England and later into Ireland, Scotland was for the most part spared. Scottish religious leaders were able to develop their own sect of Christianity free from the heavy hand of the English crown *or* the Parliament.

The Scottish Church would become the Presbyterian Church of Scotland, later spreading throughout the world.

None of these things, good or bad, would've taken place if Cromwell wouldn't have been promoted on July 2, 1644.

NEWTON AND THE APPLE

When you were in grammar/elementary school you probably first heard about the law of gravity: the force that keeps everything, including us, from flying off into space. It's also the same force that determines the orbit of the planets. You probably also learned, or maybe saw on an episode of the *School House Rock* cartoon if you're 40 or older, that the law of gravity was discovered when English scientist Isaac Newton watched an apple fall from a tree.

It's not exactly true, although the reality is that Newton did formulate the "universal law of gravitation," which directly spurred the Industrial Revolution, moving humanity onto its next phase of technological development. Newton liked to tell people that he came up with the law after watching an apple fall from a tree, but the truth is a bit more complicated.

Isaac Newton was born in 1642 to a commoner English family of some means but not without difficulties. Newton's father died before he was born and his mother later remarried a man that young Isaac didn't particularly like, but he died as well while Isaac was a teenager. The home situation meant that he was expected to work the family's small plot of land, although he had already shown intellectual promise at a young age.

During the 1600s, a university education was still very much a thing for the privileged. Universities were still off-limits to women and usually, only nobles or those on track for a career in the Church were admitted, but there were some exceptions and there's no doubt that young Newton was quite exceptional.

By the mid-1600s, Newton was working as a professional academic, teaching, writing, and conducting a multitude of experiments. He was instrumental in the development of modern calculus as well as understanding optics, but he is, of course, best known for his publication on the law of gravity.

Actually, Newton was quite a humble guy and if he were alive today, he'd be the first to tell you that he had previous scientists such as Aristotle, Galileo, and Copernicus to thank for his success. But there's no denying that Newton deserves a place with those men, if not foremost among them.

Newton's formulation of the law of gravity was a process more than an event, but the publication of his *Philosophiæ Naturalis Principia Mathematica* on July 5, 1687, which was his three-volume book that related his law of gravity, was an event like few others in the scientific world.

The monumental tome related some pretty heavy ideas, too heavy for me and this book, but the most important was his law of gravity. Newton wrote that "every particle attracts every other particle in the universe with a force that is directly proportional to the product of their masses and inversely proportional to the square of the distance between their centers."

I personally only know the very basics of physics and I would have a hard time following most of what Newton wrote, but it immediately became clear to those in the scientific community that the publication would have profound impacts on the fields of mathematics, natural science, and astronomy as well as enduring repercussions in people's everyday lives.

Newton's law of gravity is still more or less followed, although many scientists have abandoned it in favor of Einstein's relativity theory. It's important to point out, though, that Newton's gravitation is a *law*, while Einstein's relativity is still a *theory*.

The impact that the publication of Newton's *Principia* had on wider society was even greater.

Newton was the first among many scholars of the late 1600s and 1700s who would be part of the Enlightenment. The many philosophers and scientists who came after Newton, such as Locke, Hume, Voltaire, Rosseau, Hegel, and Jefferson have *Principia* to thank for being the beacon that guided them through the darkness of religious conflicts of the 1600s into the intellectual openness of the 1700s.

And the event that marked the beginning of this transition wasn't when an apple fell from a tree, as is commonly believed, but when an influential scientific book was first published in 1687.

STEAM ONCE POWERED
THE WORLD

The idea that machines could be powered by something other than raw horse or human power has intrigued humans since the dawn of civilization. The myths of different cultures tell of gods and goddesses who traveled on chariots and other vehicles that were seemingly self-propelled and although those were myths, people did try to make that a reality.

Early scholars noticed that steam seemed to have a power of its own. It bellowed and emitted a force that, if harnessed, could possibly make things move. Scientists in the 1st century CE took this concept and applied it to some of the earliest known steam-powered machines, but these were large and not very practical on a wide scale.

Then the Roman Empire collapsed, and most people were more concerned with survival and then rebuilding society than figuring out steam power.

But the idea of steam-powered machines reemerged in the 1500s and by the early 1700s, a major breakthrough took place from what would today seem an unlikely source.

In 1712, Thomas Newcomen was a Baptist preacher in England who also had a deep interest in the hard sciences. Today, many people think religion and science are irreconcilable, but in the 1700s, nearly all scientists were religious men like Thomas Newcome.

Newcome was aware of earlier attempts to harness steam power, which included the Savery steam pump. Invented by Englishman Thomas Savery in 1689, the Savery Steam pump was a piston less steam pump that was used industrially. Although the Savery pump worked well for quite a while, Thomas Newcome's "atmospheric engine" proved to be revolutionary and one of the true sparks of the Industrial Revolution (we'll get to the other one in the next story).

If you were to see Necome's invention today, you may think it was an oil pump. On one end was the boiler, filled with water and fed with coal, which powered the pump that was used to remove water from mines.

Necome's pump improved upon Savery's model by adding some key features. First, it utilized the ideas of vacuum and pressure as the way to generate the actual steam. Most importantly, it added a piston and cylinder, allowing the machine to keep working for longer periods.

Necome's steam engine was adopted throughout England and by the end of the 1700s, there were hundreds operating. The Newcome steam engine allowed England to extract coal and other minerals that it then used to power its cities and build its massive military.

It's no coincidence that England became a major imperial power in the 1700s and, perhaps even more important, it became *the* center of the economic and financial world at the time.

Although Newcome's steam engine was later made obsolete by James Watt's steam engine invention in 1776, it all began with Newcome in 1712. He ensured that steam would power the world for the next 150 years.

DID A KEY AND A KITE HARNESS THE POWER OF ELECTRICITY?

So far many of the events we've looked at in this book have been processes more than singular instances, but in every case, there's been no doubt that they happened and that they definitely left lasting impacts on the world.

So, now let's take a look at a singular event that happened very quickly - and that many people question if it even took place.

It begins with one of America's favorite founding fathers, probably the most popular one to never be president, Benjamin Franklin, and his electricity experiment that supposedly involved a kite, a key, and a storm.

First, though, it's important to understand just how Franklin was able to grasp the impact that experiment had, or if it even happened. Some people have the idea that Benjamin Franklin was a bit of a kooky old man who conducted a few experiments when he wasn't busy being a political agitator.

Nothing could be further from the truth.

Although it is true that Franklin was at the forefront of the Patriot cause before and during the American Revolution, he was one of the older leaders (he was born in 1706), so his activism tended to be a bit less fiery and more theoretical than "boots on the ground." With that said, Franklin's writings played a critical element in the philosophical reasons for American independence and his work outside the political arena was extensive and varied.

In many ways, Franklin was as much of a Renaissance man as Copernicus.

Benjamin Franklin was the US's first Postmaster General, he helped organize the Philadelphia fire department, and he was a well-respected newspaper writer and editor among other endeavors.

But it was Franklin's work in the hard sciences where he made his biggest impacts, and that's what interests us here. Franklin is credited with inventing bifocal glasses, the Franklin stove, and the lightning rod, which brings us to his famed experiment with the kite and the key.

The story begins in the 1740s when the always studious and inquisitive Franklin decided to dive into the idea of electricity. Electricity had been known to humans since ancient times, but what exactly it was and how it was created remained a mystery throughout time. When the era known as the Enlightenment began in the 1700s, scholars began cutting through some of the superstitions surrounding electricity and started publishing solid ideas based on sound experiments.

Franklin invented a multiple plate capacitor in 1748 that became the forerunner of batteries as we know them, but it was Franklin's 1752 experiment that proved to be groundbreaking.

So, let's first decide if this experiment even happened.

Franklin published the experiment in the October 19, 1752, issue of the *Pennsylvania Gazette* and it was also read to the Royal

Society in Britain on December 21, 1752, but the best description of the experiment, and the one that has produced so many recreations in fiction and pop culture, is British scientist Joseph Priestley's account. Priestley published his account in his 1767 book, *History and Present Status of Electricity.*

According to all of the accounts, the intention of Franklin's experiment was to prove lightning is electricity and that it can be harnessed, so on the afternoon of June 15, 1752, he did just that with a kite, two strings, a wire, a key, and a Leyden jar (a device that can catch and hold an electrical charge).

Aided by his son William and knowing that a thunderstorm was approaching (Franklin was also the writer of *Poor Richard's Almanac*), he went to an open field in Philadelphia to conduct his experiment.

The first thing to make clear is that the kite wasn't hit with a direct lightning strike. That would have killed Ben! No, the wire in the kite caught some of the ambient electricity from the storm, sent it down the wet string while a dry string he was holding insulated him. The charge then went through the key and into the jar.

In addition to using a dry string as an insulator and ground, Franklin stood under a roof to keep dry and avoid taking a direct lightning strike.

So, Franklin did, in fact, conduct this famous kite experiment and it was huge!

With that said, a Frenchman named Thomas-François Dalibard successfully did the same experiment a month earlier, but in the scientific world, the publication is everything, so Franklin's published accounts meant he would forever be remembered for it and Dalibard would be all but forgotten.

Franklin's kite experiment immediately had major impact on the world. He used the knowledge of the experiment to invent the lightning rod, which despite its simplicity, is still used today and has saved countless buildings from destructive lightning strikes.

But more importantly, Benjamin Franklin's kite experiment proved that electricity could be harnessed, stored, and used later. Once this was known, it opened the door for further advances that involved light, radio waves, television, and film. In other words, you could say that Benjamin Franklin's electricity experiment helped further spur the Industrial Revolution and the modern world. And it all began in a field in Philadelphia in 1752.

THE SHOT HEARD
AROUND THE WORLD

July 4 may be the national holiday in the United States and the day when Americans reflect on their country's history while cooking on the grill with family and friends, but April 19, 1775, is probably even more important in the big picture, not only of American history but for world history.

It was on that day that the American Revolution officially began when a force of 700 British soldiers left Boston, Massachusetts to retrieve a cache of weapons in the nearby town of Concord. When you look at the series of events that started on the evening of April 18 and culminated on the 19th, it's amazing to think that so many things could have happened some other way.

The British could have just walked in unopposed and grabbed all those weapons.

Paul Revere could never have made his famous "midnight ride." (By the way, the whole "British are coming" thing was added later. He was on a super-secret mission so loudly advertising what was happening would've defeated the purpose!)

American philosopher Ralph Waldo Emerson could never have written the "Concord Hymn" poem in 1837 that first made the phrase "the shot heard around the world" popular.

And most importantly, America could not have gained its independence from Britain! Or, at least, not in the 1700s and not in the way that it did, but instead in the more gradual way Canada and Australia did.

So, let's look at how and why Lexington and Concord were such important moments in the history of the world.

The great geographical distance between Britain and its 13 American colonies, as well as Canada to a certain extent, gradually began leading to distinct cultural, political, and economic differences. By the mid-1700s, the colonists still saw themselves as British, but their version of the language had begun changing, they viewed the world differently, and they weren't afraid to tell their British rulers these things. They wanted to conquer more land to the west of the Appalachian Mountains, which the British government was against, didn't have problems trading with the French or other British enemies, and most importantly, wanted direct representation in the British Parliament.

"No taxation without representation" became the mantra of people in the Patriot cause in the mid to late 1700s. As the British government enacted special taxes on the colonies, Patriots protested in several ways, one of the most spectacular being the Boston Tea Party in 1773. In that action, a group of Patriots protesting the Tea Act of 1773 boarded three ships bound for Britain and dumped the tea rather than pay the tax.

This was the infamous Tea Party that's still often used by all sides in American political discourse.

It was a minor victory for the Patriots, but also only a temporary one.

Cooler heads on both sides of the Atlantic tried to find some sort of solution for the situation in the Colonies that was looking increasingly like it could turn really bad, really fast. Anti-British violence had already occurred when the Boston Massacre took place in 1770, but the casualties were relatively low - five colonists were killed, and a small number of British soldiers were injured.

But something seemed quite different in 1774, especially in Boston. The Patriots were better organized, with the Continental Congress, and local militias were established throughout the Colonies. Things were so tense that the British didn't even bother to go to some places.

Other than Boston, Massachusetts was a no-go zone for the British - and Boston wasn't exactly friendly, either!

All of this got even worse on June 22, 1774, when the so-called "Intolerable Acts" went into effect in the American colonies. The Intolerable Acts were a number of laws that were meant to punish the colonists through a variety of sometimes well-thought-out measures.

For instance, there was the Quartering Act, which forced colonists to house British soldiers.

Then there was the Massachusetts Government Act, which essentially took away Massachusetts' colonial charter and put all government power directly in the hands of the British military, making the Bay Colony a police state.

But even with all of this happening, American independence was still not an inevitability. Americans are nothing else if not resilient, which is perhaps just a nice way of saying stubborn! Sure, they were angry, but their options were limited and overall, their best choice was staying in the British Empire. After all, they were British and despite some differences, most of them still saw the limeys as their cousins across the pond.

The key word there is *most*.

As I pointed out, Massachusetts was a virtual no-go zone for the British and the Massachusetts Government Act only made those harsh feelings in the colony even worse. So, when the Patriots learned that the British were sending a sizable force to take some guns and teach the colonists a lesson, about 4,000 colonists decided they'd had enough.

When the British forces arrived in Boston and began their march east; an event happened in the middle of the night on April 18, Paul Revere and some other Patriots met at the Old North Church in downtown Boston to put their plan into action.

The British objective was the town of Concord, which was a hotbed of Patriot activity and the sight of the supposed cache, but first, they had to pass through another Patriot town, Lexington.

The Minutemen of Lexington weren't going to let the British waltz through their town, so they came out with muskets in hand to show them what they were made of. The British easily defeated the Patriots at Lexington, though, killing eight men and wounding ten. Only one British soldier was wounded.

But the first shot had been fired and there was no going back. And by the time the British arrived at Concord, a force of about 250 Massachusetts farm boys were waiting.

A fierce battle took place on the bridge, which the Patriots won, sending the better equipped and trained British into retreat back to Boston. The British lost even more men on their march back to Boston, as they were the victim of repeated hit-and-run attacks and small-scale skirmishes.

The final casualty numbers of the Battles of Lexington and Concord weren't astonishing, even by 18th-century standards when casualty counts were never very high: 73 British were killed and 174 wounded, while 49 Patriots were killed and 39 were wounded.

The greatest impact of the battles was that it all but assured American independence would happen violently and that the new nation would form an identity that, although heavily influenced by Britain, was also quite unique. The United States would remain on the geopolitical sidelines for more than 100 years, but by the mid-20th century, it would overtake its parent as the premier world power.

The Battles of Lexington and Concord also had a tremendous impact on the way warfare was conducted.

The old standard of infantry standing in formation and slowly advancing on the opposing force continued well into the 1800s, but the type of irregular warfare many of the Patriots employed at Lexington and Concord became more common.

As important as the shot heard around the world was, perhaps the most interesting thing about it is it only happened due to a fair amount of stubbornness from both sides.

IT SEEMED LIKE A GREAT PLACE FOR A PRISON

Australia has always been a bit of an enigmatic place. Located in the Southern Hemisphere, far away from the mainland of Asia and even farther from South America, Australia was, and still is, the most isolated continent. You probably know that it's also a country, the only continent-country on Earth, which also makes it unique.

But Australia's relative isolation meant that it would develop in quite a different way than the rest of the world, even compared to other places that Europeans colonized.

Australia's isolation goes far back to before human civilization at the end of the last ice age more than 50,000 years ago. Once the water levels rose, the first nation people (aboriginals) in Australia were stuck there with a whole lot of marsupials, many of which can only be found on this continent.

Australia remained isolated for thousands of years, and even as the world was becoming smaller and more connected during the Age of Exploration of the 1500s, Australia was missed. It wasn't located on the way between the Americas and Asia, so it wasn't until the 1600s when Dutch and Spanish navigators were exploring Indonesia that it was even seen by Europeans for the first time.

It wouldn't be until the 1700s that British explorer James Cook began surveying the coast. In 1770, he claimed the continent for the British crown.

But it was such a big continent and so far from Britain that it was difficult to find anyone who would want to settle in what was perceived as an exotic, hostile land, so Thomas Townshend, the 1st Viscount Sydney, decided he'd pick a population who had no choice - convicts.

Ah yes, the 1700s was a great time if you were an ambitious British noble looking for new lands to colonize but not so great if you were a petty criminal convicted of a minor crime. In the 1700s, those convicted of minor thefts, swindles, or even debtors were routinely sent to the Americas as convicts or "indentured servants," which is just a nice way of saying "slaves."

Serious criminals, such as murderers or rapists, were usually executed, so Britain's domestic prison population remained fairly small and quite manageable.

Of course, though, as we saw in our previous story, the American Revolution made quite a few impacts on world events. In this case, it cut off a destination for Britain's prison population.

But New South Wales (which is still the name of a state in Australia) would do quite nicely.

So, by January 20, 1788, the fleet's eleven ships carrying 775 convicts, some of their family members (yes, some were allowed to bring their wives and children), some marines, sailors, and other workers had all gathered in Botany Bay in what is today Sydney.

The settlers moved a few days later to what is now Port Jackson and officially founded the colony of New South Wales on January 26, on lands inhabited by indigenous peoples for at least 60,000 years prior. The initial colonization was tough, as Australia was so far from Britain, and trade routes in general, that it made getting supplies there difficult.

Australians had to quickly learn how to be self-sufficient, and the convicts and non-convicts had to learn how to cooperate and live with each other.

The idea of sending convicts to Australia and using them as a sort of vanguard of colonization proved to be so successful that other convict colonies were established in New South Wales and eventually in Queensland, Tasmania, Victoria, and Western Australia. The last convict ship landed in Australia in 1868, and by that time, the policy had shaped "Down Under" and eventually the world.

Australian society developed in a way that was totally Western and British in many ways. Yet like in the United States, it also had its unique flavor. Convicts who completed their sentences usually stayed in Australia and in many communities, they lived more or less freely among non-convicts while they did their sentences. This helped to break down many of the class distinctions that were so apparent and even promoted, back in Britain. Australians didn't really care if a person (one in seven convicts were women) they were working with, or neighbors with, was a convict.

The convict character of Australia's foundation also helped create the country's rugged, individualist character that has come to define it today.

And after decades of being embarrassed about their origins, by the mid-1900s Australians began embracing their tough origins and their uniqueness from their British cousins. Today, about 20% of all Australians have "convict" ancestry. Some Australians celebrate their country's origins every year on January 26, Australia Day (their official national holiday).

DID SHE REALLY SAY, "LET THEM EAT CAKE"?

Our next story brings us to the lifestyles of the rich and infamous in history and how, often enough, a lack of self-awareness can have tragic consequences. But let's first briefly go back to the American Revolution and the role the French played in it.

Today, the French may get a bad rap for a lot of things in the US, from some of their food to their tastes in art, but the reality is they played a huge role in the American Revolution. In fact, the American Revolution probably wouldn't have been successful without French support.

French philosophers like Voltaire and Rosseau wrote about many of the ideas the Founding Fathers advocated, and French culture, in general, was loved by the Founders. Most of the Founders spoke French, knew all the latest French dances, and their wives loved the French fashions.

But more importantly, the French Army supported the Continental Army on the ground and was vital to the ultimate American victory at the Battle of Yorktown in 1781.

Yet for all the French support for American liberty, things weren't always that way back home.

France was a monarchy, ruled by King Louis XVI and his young Austrian-born wife, Queen Marie Antoinette. Despite being a king, Louis began his rule as a bit of a reformer, but pressure from the nobles forced him into an unwinnable position. Supporting Americans actually didn't help either, as it put the country into debt, and when combined with crop failure and famine, France was ripe for revolution in 1789.

But the French Revolution proved to be nothing like the American Revolution.

In many ways, the American Revolution was very "civil", at least as much as a war can be, and after the war, the reprisals against British loyalists were minimal. The French Revolution proved to be much more brutal and partisan, with the revolutionaries violently attempting to eliminate all signs of the old order.

This is where the truth, or not, of Marie Antoinette's "let them eat cake" quote and its potential impact on the world comes in.

Let's begin with the veracity of the infamous quote. There's no documented evidence that the queen said it, but at the same time, there is no evidence that she *didn't*. Based on what we know about Marie's lifestyle and her attitude, she very well could've uttered those fateful words.

Marie Antoinette was born in 1755 into the royal Hapsburg family of the Austro-Hungarian Empire, which meant that she was immediately part of the privileged 1% of the era, and more like the 0.5%.

At the tender age of 14, Marie married the future Louis XVI of France in what was a marriage of power and convenience. Under normal circumstances, the marriage probably would have been fine, and the young Marie could have enjoyed being a queen in peace, but times were rapidly changing. When revolutionary rumblings broke out in 1783, the queen just wasn't prepared for it.

It's important to remember that Marie Antoinette was still a girl when she became one of the most powerful women in the world. She liked wearing nice clothes, attending balls, and even still playing with dolls when she was the queen. So, it's not an understatement to say that this young, beautiful girl was in over her head!

As the people of France rebelled, Louis XVI appeared weak and feckless, while Marie was often viewed by the people as cold and uncaring. That's how the "let them eat cake" quote started.

Eventually, the mob descended on the royal palace, arrested the royal couple, and then executed them by guillotine, first Louis on January 21, 1793, and then Marie on October 16, 1793.

Marie Antoinette and Louis XVI's executions created many political waves that rippled through the world for decades.

The most immediate effect was that the French Revolution took an even more violent turn in what became known as the Reign of Terror from 1793 to 1794. Thousands of "enemies" of the Revolution lost their heads while thousands more languished in prisons.

The Reign of Terror was finally ended by conservatives within the Revolution, which then paved the way for none other than Napoleon Bonaparte to come to power, thrusting all of Europe into war for the next two decades.

HOW THE BRITISH NAVY ESTABLISHED ITS SUPREMACY

Speaking of Napoleon, when the little guy came to power, it had more than a few major impacts on world history. Napoleon became the First Consul of France in 1799, which was basically the president and at that time, dictator, before making himself Emperor of the French in 1804. Even before Napoleon was the supreme ruler of France, though, he was engaged in a series of wars for control of Europe.

The Napoleonic Wars (1803-1815) are so-called because they were a series of wars that pitted Napoleon against the rest of Europe. Really, it was a series of wars between Napoleon and the British.

Napoleon had developed the greatest land force the world had ever seen, while the British ruled the waves. The modern British Navy actually began during the reign of Henry VIII. When Henry wasn't busy killing his wives, searching for a new wife, or fighting against the Catholic Church, he dedicated a fair number of resources to the British Navy.

By the late 1500s, the British Navy was on par with the Spanish and Portuguese and in the 1700s, it was the number one naval force in the world.

With that said, it still wasn't truly *dominant*.

The French had enough able admirals, sailors, and resources to give the British problems, as they did during the American Revolution, and the Spanish were still relatively strong on the seas.

But all of that changed in one earthshattering Naval engagement on October 21, 1805.

This important moment in history really began months earlier, as the British used their naval dominance to blockade the Atlantic coastline to prevent the French and their Spanish allies from doing an amphibious invasion of England. Napoleon knew that he couldn't decisively defeat the British on the high seas, but if he got his Grand Army (as it was called) to British soil, it wouldn't matter. But for that to happen, he needed the French and Spanish navies to break the British blockade.

First, Napoleon had to get his navy out of the Mediterranean Sea, which was no easy task because top British Admiral Horatio Nelson was searching for them. The French fleet, which was led by Admiral Pierre-Charles Villeneuve, successfully evaded the British and sailed through the Strait of Gibraltar where they rendezvoused with the Spanish fleet and sailed to the Caribbean, hoping to throw the British off.

But Nelson followed them all the way to the Caribbean and back to Europe. When the fleets made it back to Europe in July, they were to begin the amphibious operation. Once again, destiny got in the way.

Villeneuve failed to make it to France in August to meet Napoleon, which meant that the emperor had to take his war-weary troops into Germany for battle. If he hadn't, the men may have just gone home - or worse, they may have mutinied. Seeing an opening, Nelson ended his relief time in England early, gathered the fleet, and sailed south to Spain to confront the French and Spanish fleets of the Cape of Trafalgar on October 21, 1805.

Based on numbers alone, there's no way the French and Spanish should've lost the battle.

They had 33 "ships of the line" (what war ships were called during that era) versus 27 for the British. And the French and Spanish sailors and marines were a fairly seasoned force at that point, so the British had no experience advantage.

But oftentimes in war, when all things are equal, it comes down to the commanders and in that respect, the British had the upper hand.

Admiral Nelson knew the only way to overcome the French-Spanish numerical superiority was to divide their fleet into smaller parts, which he did, heroically leading the charge in his ship.

Villeneuve told Spanish Admiral Frederico Carlos Gravina before the battle that a British frontal assault was a real possibility, but for some reason, neither of the admirals made any plans to counter it.

Nelson's charge won the day, although he was killed in the battle. Gravina sustained wounds that he later died from, and Villeneuve was captured by the British. The French-Spanish fleet had 21 of their ships of the line captured, while the British didn't lose any ships. More than 4,000 French and Spanish sailors and marines were killed in the battle compared to only 458 British.

The Battle of Trafalgar marked the beginning of the end of Napoleon's goal of global domination. He continued to win battles on the continent for several years, but as we'll see in the next story, even those involved small margins of error when the British controlled the high seas, and the French and Spanish navies were nearly destroyed.

British rule on the waters was assured not just for the remainder of the Napoleonic Wars, but for the next 100 plus years. Britain was able to take its new naval dominance to nearly every corner of the world in the 1800s, enjoying its greatest period of influence and power.

Horatio Nelson became one of the most famous and popular personalities in English history as a result of his sacrifice and later had the famous square in London named after him.

As for Villeneuve?

Well, he lived in England on parole for several months before he was allowed to return to France. He attempted to rejoin the military but was given the cold shoulder. Then on April 22, 1806, his lifeless body was found in a hotel room in Rennes, France. He had died from six stab wounds to his chest, which suggests foul play, but a farewell letter was found in the room addressed to his wife.

The government ruled Villeneuve's death a suicide. Um…yeah, sure!

NAPOLEON WAS GOOD, BUT NOT THAT GOOD

Napoleon may not have been the biggest guy around physically, but his influence, personality, and ego made him a giant among men. There's no doubt that Napoleon was one of the most important people in the world in the late 1700s and early 1800s, if not *the* most important person of that era, which is why the previous two stories in our book, and this one, concern him either directly or indirectly.

And this one is the most important.

After France's loss at the Battle of Trafalgar, Napoleon had to face the reality that he wasn't going to invade England any time soon. Even worse, Britain controlled the high seas, which meant that getting resources in and out of continental Europe would be extremely difficult.

So, in 1806, Napoleon responded by forming the "Continental System", which was essentially all of the countries of Europe except Britain, Portugal, and some of the smaller Balkan states. The goal of the Continental System was to fight fire with fire by installing an embargo against Britain.

The embargo hurt the Continental System countries more than Britain, so by 1810, there were rumblings within the system that could only be quieted by Napoleon's threats. On December 31, 1810, Alexander I, the Tsar of Russia, had enough of Napoleon's threats and switched sides.

So, Napoleon did what he knew how to do best and gathered his Grand Army to prepare for an invasion of Russia. His French forces, combined with German and Polish allies, numbered between 500,000 and 600,000 men. But not only was the Continental Army large, but it was also the best equipped, trained, and skilled army of the era. In fact, it was arguably the most formidable army in the history of the world.

Yes, the French were truly badasses in the early 1800s!

Napoleon left allied Poland with his Grand Army on June 24, 1812, believing he had more than enough time to march to Moscow, teach the Tsar a thing or two, and march back to Poland or Prussia before winter. He knew that although the Russians could field an army of similar size, they were far outmatched by the Grand Army.

But Napoleon soon found out that Russian soldiers weren't his army's biggest threat.

Napoleon underestimated the vast size of Russia and the problems it posed for his army's logistics. They traveled for days at a time without seeing a soul and the way was often arduous: forests, swamps, rivers, and a lack of roads meant that they didn't arrive in the outskirts of Moscow until September 7.

The Grand Army defeated the Russians at the Battle of Borodino and gained control of Moscow, but the city was a ghost town. The Russians wisely evacuated the city before the French arrived and left nothing for the victors - no food, clothing, or even wood for fires.

The Grand Army then began its long journey back to friendly territory, which is when things started to get really ugly.

Russian peasants, soldiers, and Cossacks performed ambush attacks on the Grand Army during its westward march, reducing its numbers through gradual attrition. And when the Grand Army soldiers weren't on guard for guerilla attacks, they were dying of starvation or freezing to death. The Grand Army soldiers eventually ate all their horses (some have argued that this is how horse meat became popular in France) and when they were done with them, they actually ate their coats, boots, and anything else that could fill their stomachs, too!

And then winter came early to the region, bringing heavy snow and freezing temperatures.

By the time the Grand Army finally made it into friendly territory, about half its number had died, primarily from starvation and hypothermia. About another 100,000 were either captured or deserted.

I can't say I blame them.

The impact of Napoleon's ill-fated 1812 invasion of Russia was catastrophic for him and his empire. It was all downhill for Napoleon after Russia, as his severely decimated army lost battle after battle. Eventually, the members of the Continental System began abandoning France. Then even the French began turning on Napoleon.

Napoleon abdicated his throne in 1814 and was exiled to the Mediterranean island of Elba, although in 1815 he attempted a comeback of sorts. Napoleon's final defeat was at the Battle of Waterloo on June 18, 1815, which is the origin of the term "Waterloo," meaning a person's demise.

In reality, Napoleon's true Waterloo took place in the fall and early winter of 1812 in the vast expanse of European Russia.

TWO WARS FOUGHT
FOR DRUG DEALERS

Since the 1970s, the US government, as well as many other governments around the world, have supposedly fought a "War on Drugs." I say supposedly because not much headway ever seems to be made and in recent years, things have only gotten worse with the explosion of legal, pharmaceutical opioids. The opioid scourge has left a wide swath of destruction in many communities across middle America and doesn't show any signs of improving.

To many, it seems as though the government's War on Drugs is words at best.

But some have taken that thinking a step further and accused the government, or at least some agencies within it, of actively trafficking drugs. There's plenty of evidence that the CIA, or members of the CIA, trafficked heroin out of Southeast Asia in the 1970s and cocaine from Latin America in the 1980s, in convert operations that they would never admit to.

After all, no government would ever publicly admit trafficking drugs, right?

Wrong!

For our next history-changing event, we travel to mid-1800s China. If you remember, the British Empire was at its peak and one of its jewels was India. India produced spices, tea, and opium for the British. Yes, opium, is the natural substance that provides the basis for today's deadly opioid drugs.

Opium was more or less legal back then, but its use was generally frowned upon by polite society and the elites of Western countries, so it wasn't readily available in most places. It was prescribed by doctors, often as laudanum, but its recreational use was uncommon and relegated to some of the darkest corners of the big cities. But plenty was grown in India, so industrious British merchants decided to ship huge amounts of it to China, where it became very popular - and a very big problem.

In response, the emperor of China's Qing Dynasty outlawed opium and even ordered Chinese soldiers to seize shipments of it in the ports.

This didn't sit well with British merchants, who were very influential in the British government, so the mighty British Navy went to China and on September 4, 1839, went to war over its people's "right" to sell opium to the Chinese.

Yes, you read that correctly. The British went to war on behalf of drug dealers!

The First Opium War, as it became known, ended on August 29, 1842, with a resounding British victory. The most obvious impact was that the British took control of Hong Kong as a colony until 1997.

The British victory also allowed them to import some opium into China, but most ports remained off-limits until they defeated the Qing Dynasty once more in the Second Opium War (1856-1860).

The Second Opium War opened up all of China for British opium imports and institutionalized the idea of "treaty ports." Treaty ports were coastal cities where Western powers could buy and sell their goods duty-free. They effectively became controlled by the Western powers and were quasi-colonies that existed well into the 20th century.

Needless to say, the Chinese never liked the treaty ports much, which was one of the primary reasons behind the Boxer Rebellion (1899-1901).

The Opium Wars also impacted nearby Japan but in quite a different way.

When the Americans forced Japan to open itself to the world in 1854, the latter did so more or less enthusiastically after seeing what had just happened to China. Once Japan established a Western-style government in 1868 and modernized its military and economy, it somewhat ironically joined the Western powers by taking part in the control of some Chinese treaty ports.

Another impact the Opium Wars had was the dispersing of Chinese people throughout the world. One of the demands of the Western Powers in the Second Opium War was the ability to hire cheap Chinese laborers, which they called "coolies." These laborers made their way to places such as Canada, Australia, South Africa, and the United States, where they helped build the railroads across those countries.

Unfortunately, opium addiction also followed many of these Chinese workers.

CALIFORNIA WAS
A BACKWATER BEFORE 1848

Many of those Chinese "coolies" were brought to the western United States, particularly California, where they worked in the gold mines and also helped build the railroads. But before all that happened, California had to enter the modern world, which basically took place in one moment.

As unique as California is today, it was even more so before the 1840s. California began as the province of Alta California (Upper California) in the colony of New Spain. When Mexico won its independence from Spain in 1821 it became Mexican territory, but it remained relatively underdeveloped.

California was separated from the rest of Mexico by mountains and desert, making land travel a challenge. Getting to California by ship from Mexico City took weeks as well, as it involved a land trip from the capital city to the Pacific Ocean and then sailing around Baja Mexico before going north to California.

And getting there from the United States was even tougher.

Adventurous American souls who wanted to visit or move to California had two options: an overland journey across the desert and mountains of the west or sailing south around the tip of South America before sailing north again.

The first option was quite dangerous for many reasons. From hostile Indian tribes to inclement weather and harsh elements, travelers were very much on their own. The second option could also be dangerous, but it was also expensive.

Still, many Americans did make the journey to California and by 1846, there was a sizable Anglo-American population in the region. The American settlers set up stores, trapped fur, and farmed the land in the fertile Central Valley, which was available at low prices.

California's future took a drastic turn on April 25, 1846, when the Mexican-American War began. The war was basically about unsettled issues between Texas and Mexico after the Texas War of Independence, but it involved the entire northwestern section of Mexico, and what would become the American southwest.

Anglo Californians rebelled against the Mexican government and ultimately took control. California later became part of the United States after the Mexican-American War ended and the Mexican Cession ceded what is now the American southwest, including California, to the US on February 2, 1848.

But just about a week before that, something even bigger happened in California that immediately thrust it from a backwater province to the most important territory, and then state, in the US.

On January 24, a man named James Marshall was hard at work building a mill for John (Johann) Sutter on the American River in the scenic Sierra Nevada Mountains in northern California. It began just like any other day, with Marshall checking the river, except this time he noticed distinct shining specks that could only be gold.

He was right, it was gold!

News of the discovery at Sutter's Mill spread like wildfire around the world, bringing fortune hunters, adventurers, and entrepreneurs to California by the thousands. A wave of American and European immigrants poured into California, followed by a smaller trickle of Chinese immigrants, giving the territory the boost to the population it needed to become a state overnight. On September 9, 1850, California was admitted as the 31st State in the American Union.

Perhaps most importantly for the time, California was admitted as a free state. California's ban on slavery meant that it would fight on the side of the "North" during the Civil War and when combined with its relative isolation, it would ensure that the state would develop a unique identity.

California's early commitment to risk-taking, entrepreneurship, individualism, and political freedom and equality - not to mention its good weather - contributed to it being a destination for Americans and non-Americans. In many ways, the emergence of the film and aerospace industries, as well as the explosion of Silicon Valley, can all trace their origins to the discovery of gold at Sutter's Mill in 1848.

1848: A YEAR
OF REVOLUTION

Let's go back to continental Europe, but keep things in 1848, and take a look at another major impact that the collapse of Napoleon's empire had on the continent. For better or worse, Napoleon united Europe under his rule but once he was vanquished, there was a major power vacuum. He had overthrown many of the monarchies, the most important of which was the Holy Roman Empire (remember that one?).

Another ironic impact of Napoleon's conquests was that although he conquered and ruled over non-French peoples, he still outwardly professed to uphold the ideals of the French Revolution, one of which was the right to national self-government. So, it was no coincidence that after the French Empire collapsed, people all over Europe began thinking of new types of governments.

Monarchy was out and democracy was in…!

A number of different "isms" also became cool by the mid-1800s, especially nationalism and socialism.

German-speaking people began to see themselves as Germans more than as subjects of the different kingdoms they lived in, and the same was true among Italians who lived in many different kingdoms and republics similar to the Germans.

And by this time, the Industrial Revolution was in full swing. Urban workers, who often toiled long hours in harsh conditions for little pay, began to see socialism as a viable political alternative, especially after Karl Marx published his *Communist Manifesto* in February 1848.

Strikes and riots broke out in February in France that eventually brought down the government, putting Louis Napoleon Bonaparte (the nephew of *the* Napoleon) into office as France's first president in December 1848.

But as was the case with French politics in that era, and apparently with the Bonaparte family, Louis liked the power, so he stayed in office after his term in 1851 and then proclaimed himself Emperor of the French, Napoleon III, in 1852.

Well, so much for the democratic revolution in France!

The 1848 revolution affected nearly every country in Western Europe, but in the German and Italian kingdoms and republics, they took on a nationalistic tone. Workers and nationalists hit the streets together in the German-speaking and Italian-speaking lands in March 1848 with the ultimate goal of unifying their countries under one government. Although the nationalist revolutions were not successful in 1848, they set the stage for success decades later in Germany and Italy.

Uprisings in Austria were suppressed, and the monarchy survived, while in Hungary the people were initially successful at overthrowing their Hapsburg-Austrian rulers. The Austrian monarchy eventually defeated the Hungarian nationalists and put the country under a military dictatorship, but it wouldn't last.

In 1867, the Austrians agreed to share power with the Hungarians in a double monarchy arrangement, giving birth to the Austro-Hungarian Empire.

The 1848 revolution was most successful in Denmark, where the absolute monarchy was replaced with the constitutional monarchy it has today.

Most of the 1848 revolutions may have failed, but the impact they had on Europe and the world continued for decades. The old monarchies may have won most of those initial battles, but democracy and republicanism prevailed in the long run, with more and more countries gradually moving from absolute monarchy to constitutional monarchy.

The idea of nationalism was also a big winner, as it led to Germany and Italy unifying and continued to be a popular ideology through the world wars.

Socialism and communism also spread from Europe to the rest of the world after 1848 and became quite popular in some places (we'll get to a couple of those later). Today, most people know who Karl Marx is, but that might not have happened if the strikes, riots, and revolts didn't kick off in 1848.

A VOTE FOR CIVIL WAR

If you live in the United States or follow American politics, then you've certainly heard the phrase "this is the most important presidential election in US history" uttered at least once during the last two presidential elections. This may, in fact, be true, but the reality is we won't know that until some point in the future. Actually, there's a good chance *we* personally never will know it, because if there's one thing this book should have shown you by now, it's that the biggest events and moments in history aren't usually recognized as such until sometime later.

Today, we know that the presidential election of 1860 *was* the most important election in American history. It decided the type of country the United States would be and directly led to the costliest war in American history.

So, let's take a look a closer look at this election and the impact it had on history.

To understand the impact of the 1860 election, we have to go back a bit. In some ways, we could go all the way back to Jamestown and the Pilgrims. Those two colonies represent two visions of early America that although sharing many features, also had some notable differences.

Both of those early colonies believed in a combination of community and individualism and were also Christian, though their interpretations of the Christian faith were different.

Perhaps the biggest difference between these two early American colonies was slavery.

The Pilgrims never practiced slavery and slavery was very rare in the northeastern colonies. Farmers in New England and the northeast owned small tracts of land on which it would have been impractical and too expensive to use slaves, and many of the people of that region were also morally opposed to slavery.

Jamestown had slaves from the start and slavery became indispensable to the tobacco farmers of Virginia and Maryland and the indigo farmers of the Carolinas. Later, after Independence, as Americans moved west, slaves became key in the labor of large southern cotton plantations.

In the Northwest (what is now known as the Midwest), immigrants from Scandinavia, Ireland, the German-speaking kingdoms, and the American northeast farmed smaller plots of land where families did all the labor, or they sometimes hired hands.

So, the struggle between slave states and free states was set pretty early in American history, but political compromises in 1820 and 1850 kept things from getting out of hand. It also helped that the two major political parties from 1828 to 1852 - the Whigs and the Democrats - didn't differ much on the slavery issue.

All of that changed when the Republican Party was formed in 1854.

The Republicans tapped into a combination of issues that the other two parties were ignoring. Regarding immigration, the Republicans took a tough stance, drawing members from the new American Party, but it was the slavery issue that made the Republicans, and Abraham Lincoln, a national power.

Lincoln became a household name during his failed 1858 senate bid in Illinois, where he debated incumbent Democrat Senator Stephen Douglas at a series of locations around the state. Lincoln did well in the debates, establishing himself as an excellent public speaker, a man of sharp intellect despite his humble background, and a leader of the national Republican Party. And in fairness to Lincoln, US senators were chosen by the state legislatures at that time, not directly as they are today.

The most important part of Lincoln's political platform, which was synonymous with the Republican Party's platform, was the idea that slavery was evil. It's important to point out that he didn't necessarily believe in racial equality, but he did believe slavery was a scourge to everyone involved.

This idea resonated well with farmers in the North who saw slave labor as competition, as well as abolitionists who opposed slavery on moral grounds.

So, when Lincoln became the Republican Party's nomination for president in 1860, many in the South took that as an ominous sign. Lincoln may have publicly said he was only against the spread of slavery and wouldn't do anything to stop it in the states where it already existed, but many Southerners thought they knew better.

But what could they do?

Well, in 1860 there was always the option of voting, but the problem was the numbers didn't add up. Even if all the slave states voted in a single bloc for Southern Democrat John Breckinridge, they would only have 123 electoral votes versus the 180 the Northern states, California, and Oregon would give Lincoln. But to further complicate things, Stephen Douglas ran as a moderate Democrat and won Missouri, while John Bell ran as the Constitutional Party's nominee and won Tennessee, Kentucky, and Virginia.

Lincoln won with 180 electoral votes, but just under 40% of the popular vote. But as supporters of Hilary Clinton, or Donald Trump, will tell you, it's the electoral vote that matters in US presidential elections.

Most Americans knew that a vote for Lincoln was probably a vote for Civil War. South Carolina became the first state to secede from the Union on December 20, 1860, and it was followed by eight other Southern states in the months before Confederate forces attacked the US naval base at Fort Sumter, South Carolina on April 12, 1861.

The American Civil War officially began on that day, but most at the time knew it all really began on election day, November 6, 1860.

KILLING LINCOLN DIDN'T
HELP THE SOUTHERN CAUSE

On April 14, 1865, the Civil War was winding down and it was only a matter of time until the Union won. How they won was perhaps even more important. It's been said by military experts that winning a war is one thing, but winning peace is an entirely different matter.

You don't have to look far for recent examples of this.

During the 1960s and '70s, the US won most of the major battles in the Vietnam War, but they were never able to "win the peace" by eliminating all resistance. The same thing happened to the Soviets in Afghanistan during the 1980s and the Americans in Afghanistan from the 2000s to 2021. I could give many more examples from ancient times to the present, where an army won a war convincingly on the battlefield but had an extremely difficult time controlling things after.

As the Civil War was coming to an end, Lincoln was being pulled from two sides. On one side was the faction in the Republican Party known as the "Radical Republicans." The Radical Republicans believed that the South should pay heavily for starting the war - economically, culturally, and politically - which included disenfranchising anyone even remotely connected to the Confederacy, enfranchising newly freed slaves, taking over Southern industry, and putting most of the South under martial law.

On the other side were more moderate Republicans and what was left of the Democrat Party in the North. They urged Lincoln to pursue a more conciliatory path after the war. Remember, Lincoln was not very liberal on racial issues, to begin with, so by all accounts, he was fine with allowing the old guard to keep power in the Southern states, but without slavery and provided they re-pledge their allegiance to the United States.

Of course, there are more details but that's about the gist of it, with Lincoln heavily favoring the more moderate course, which is what makes what happened on April 14, 1865, that much more pointless and futile.

It was on that evening, at about 10:15 p.m., that Lincoln was watching a production of *Our American Cousin* with his wife, US Army Major Henry Rathbone, and Rathbone's fiancé, Clara Harris at the Ford Theatre in Washington, DC. As the couples were enjoying their evening, actor and Confederate sympathizer John Wilkes Booth silently crept in behind Lincoln, fired a shot from a pistol into the president's head, and jumped from the balcony to the stage.

Booth first yelled the Latin phrase *Sic semper tyrannis!* ("Thus, always to tyrants!") before shouting in English, "The South is avenged," or something similar. He then ran from the theater.

The thing is, though, the South wasn't "avenged" with Booth's act; in fact, he just managed to make things worse.

Booth and his fellow conspirators were quickly caught and executed. The investigation eventually resulted in the arrest and imprisonment of several other people besides the four assassins and would-be assassins: the plan was also to kill Vice President Andrew Johnson and Secretary of State William Seward.

Johnson's would-be assassin lost his nerve and got drunk, while the hit on Seward was botched.

Booth didn't exactly put together Ocean's 11 for the job, but the fact that they even thought it would somehow alleviate the South's self-induced plight points to their lack of critical thinking skills.

When Lincoln died from his wounds the next morning, it ensured that the complete opposite of what the assassins hoped for would happen. Voters in the North, who at first took a moderate attitude toward the South, voted for Radical Republicans after Lincoln's assassination, giving them control of Congress in 1866.

From there, things moved pretty quickly.

The Radical Republicans impeached President Johnson and supported Ulysses Grant's nomination as the Republican candidate for President in 1868. And since the Democrat Party was virtually eliminated until the 1870s, he was assured to be the president.

Grant then went along with the Radical Republicans' plan of Reconstruction for his first term, but later soured on it and took a moderate approach. Still, the assassination of Abraham Lincoln was one of the most pivotal events of the 1800s in large part because it had the opposite effect of what the assassins intended.

THE WAR THAT CHANGED
SOUTH AMERICA FOREVER

As the American Civil War was winding down, the War of the Triple Alliance, or the Paraguayan War (1864-1870), was just getting started in South America. American or European newspapers at the time didn't give the War of the Triple Alliance too much attention because it wasn't taking place in Europe and North America. Even today, most people know little to nothing about the war; again, not because it wasn't important, but more so due to its location.

But make no mistake, the War of the Triple Alliance played an extremely important role in modern world history for many reasons that were due in large part to it being the continent's deadliest war in history and per capita among the deadliest wars in modern history.

If you go back a bit in our encyclopedia. you'll remember that Spain and Portugal "discovered," conquered, and colonized South America. The pope had the two Catholic countries agree to their spheres of influence under the 1494 Treaty of Tordesillas, which effectively split South America, with the Portuguese getting everything east of a meridian and the Spanish everything west of it.

90

The Spanish ended up with most of South America and the Portuguese got what would become Brazil. This is why Brazil is the only Portuguese-speaking country in South America, but I guess that's a bonus event in our book. Let's get back to the 1800s!

So, as the Spanish and Portuguese empires faded in significance in the late 1700s and early 1800s, many revolutionaries in South America, such as Simon Bolivar, Antonio Jose de Sucre, Jose de San Martin, and others looked to the United States for political inspiration. These men thought, "if the Americans can do it, so can we," so they too led revolutionary movements throughout South America with varying degrees of success.

Paraguay became an independent republic in 1811, followed by Argentina in 1816, and Uruguay in 1828. Brazil followed a slightly different path, declaring its independence from Portugal in 1822 but as a New World monarchy.

Collectively, Paraguay, Uruguay, Argentina, and southern Brazil (as well as Chile) are often called the "Southern Cone," because they represent a distinct region and sub-culture within South America.

But it definitely was a rocky road getting to that point.

Almost immediately, the four countries quarreled over borders and access to the Rio de la Plata and other rivers in the region. River access was especially important to the landlocked Paraguay.

Things began to get a bit heated after Brazil started muscling in on Uruguay, invading in 1851, 1854, and finally in 1864, which proved to be the start of the region-wide War of the Triple Alliance. Tiny Paraguay was against Brazil's continued actions in

Uruguay and was actually the first to attack and declare war on Brazil on December 13, 1864.

The early phase of the war went quite well for Paraguay, with the diminutive nation winning several battles and taking some land in Uruguay.

But once Argentina decided to join Brazil and Uruguay. It would be like the US, Russia, and Mexico teaming up to beat up Canada today! Paraguay was just so far outmatched in terms of men and resources that they could never hope to win a war of attrition.

At the height of the war, Paraguay could field a maximum of about 150,000 men against Brazil's 200,000, Argentina's 30,000, and Uruguay's 5,500. Due to their vast size and production capabilities, Brazil and Argentina also had access to even more men and supplies and could easily get more supplies from the US and Europe through their ports.

Paraguay was hopelessly landlocked and unable to get more men or resources.

Once the Allies began using their numerical superiority to relentlessly push the scrappy Paraguayans deeper into their country and closer to their capital of Asuncion through 1865 and 1866, Paraguayan president and general, Francisco Solano Lopez, was ready to talk. But he considered the Allies' terms insulting, and that's a big no-no in the land where machismo and a man's word are sometimes all that matters.

So, the fighting continued until the Allies took Asuncion in January 1869 and installed a puppet government.

And that's when things got really bloody.

President Lopez fled to the hills and jungles of Paraguay and organized a guerilla resistance. The resistance continued until

Lopez was killed on March 1, 1870. Once the smoke of the war had cleared, the smell of death remained, as did the destruction of the entire nation of Paraguay.

The Triple Alliance didn't win the war through any grand strategy or superiority on the battlefield but through its numerical superiority and its willingness to be exceptionally brutal. The more the Paraguayans resisted, the more of them died, including many civilians.

It's estimated that about 70% of Paraguay's total population died during the war, up to 300,000 total. Some studies estimated that up to 90% of Paraguay's male population perished in the war, leading some scholars to call the War of the Triple Alliance one of the modern world's worst cases of genocide.

Brazil suffered the most casualties out of the Allies, with about 50,000 of its soldiers killed or wounded and an unverified 500,000 – 600,000 of its civilians killed or wounded. Argentina suffered 18,000 soldiers and 13,000 civilian casualties, while 3,100 Uruguayan soldiers died.

Overall, the War of the Triple Alliance destroyed Paraguay and left it far underdeveloped compared to its Southern Cone neighbors.

Brazil gained plenty of prestige and power in the region after the war, but debts incurred because of it seriously hurt its economy in the long run. A disproportionate number of Black freemen and slaves fought on the Brazilian side, which is cited as a major reason for Brazil banning slavery in 1888.

Brazil and Argentina also changed their immigration laws to favor a pro-European format similar to the United States in that era. With so many men dead or permanently wounded after the war, and the loss of slave labor in Brazil's case, both countries enticed European workers and farmers to emigrate from Germany, Italy, Russia, Portugal, and Spain, among other places, eventually helping to make the Southern Cone the unique region that it is today.

ONE GERMANY

Earlier we discussed the role nationalism played in the 1848 revolts across Europe, and the nation that would become Germany was ground zero of that movement. It took several decades, but eventually, Germany became a unified country, more or less, which had major repercussions for Europe and the rest of the world.

Before we dive right into Germany's unification and birth as a modern nation, let's go back a bit. If you'll remember, there was no "Germany" as a unified state for most of world history. The term "Germany" is actually derived from the Roman name for the region, Germania, which stuck in the minds of non-Germans ever since.

Of course, the Germans referred to themselves as Deutsch and Germany as Deutschland, but that's a story for another book.

You'll also remember that most of the medieval German-speaking kingdoms formed a confederation known as the Holy Roman Empire and that Napoleon destroyed it during his conquests, but also unwittingly uncorked the idea of nationalism from the bottle of European discontent.

German nationalism was defeated in 1848, but it continued to be popular. There were two things missing, though; a strong leader and an army behind that leader that could make a nation a reality.

For a time, it appeared that maybe Austria would produce that leader. The royal Hapsburg family that ruled Austria were ethnic Germans and they had plenty of resources and a large army. However, they just didn't have a charismatic leader who could appeal to the people in all the smaller German-speaking kingdoms and republics.

Then a man named Otto von Bismarck made his mark on the world.

Bismarck was born on 1 April 1815 to a noble family in the province of Saxony, which was ruled by the German-speaking Kingdom of Prussia. Although Bismarck was a noble, he understood the masses better than anyone and he learned how to successfully navigate the new bureaucratic and political structure that had been added to Prussia's existing monarchy.

In 1862, Wilhelm I, the King of Prussia, appointed Bismarck as Minister President and Foreign Minister, essentially making him the most powerful man in the kingdom. Bismarck was on a straight trajectory to the top after that, playing into the people's nationalist desires with his famous 1862 "Blood and Iron" speech and dealing with the other German-speaking kingdoms with a policy that became known as *realpolitik*.

Bismarck used realpolitik and blood and iron to forge a German Confederation led by Prussia. Prussia had a long military history (its army came up with those cool spiked helmets!) so they were best suited to lead German unification and could be the sword Bismarck needed to unify the German people.

First Prussia had to defeat Denmark in 1864 to get control of German-speaking Schleswig-Holstein, before going to war against Austria in 1866.

The Austro-Prussian War was basically a contest to see which kingdom would lead the unification process. When Prussia won on July 22, 1866, Austria was sidelined from the process and Prussia moved on to bigger and better things.

But France was the final hurdle to German unification.

Although *the* Napoleon was gone, Napoleon III was the Emperor of France in 1870, and France was still the most powerful continental European power. Many people in France wanted to curtail Prussia's growing influence, while Bismarck knew that increased tensions and possibly even war with France would only stoke German nationalism even more, thus making him and Prussia even stronger.

The French began the Franco-Prussian War on July 2, 1870, when they attacked the German city of Saarbrücken. The French gained a minor victory, but it fanned the flames of German nationalism by unifying most Germans against France.

After that, it was all downhill for the French.

The Germans captured Paris on January 28, 1871, but the war was over before that. The Germans captured Napoleon III on September 1, 1870, and on January 18, 1871, just as they were about to take Paris, the German princes, generals, and other political leaders gathered at the Palace of Versailles just outside Paris to proclaim a united German Empire ruled by Wilhelm.

This was huge.

The unified German state would later become known as the Second Reich (empire), which lasted until after World War I. After unification, Germany replaced France as the primary European continental power and a sense of enmity began between the two countries that lasted through World War II.

THE DISCOVERY OF DIAMONDS IN SOUTH AFRICA

Not long after the California Gold Rush happened, another type of mineral rush took place across the world in South Africa. In the mid-1800s, South Africa was a collection of colonies that were more or less ruled by the British.

It's important to emphasize "more or less."

The British may have had firm control over the western coastal area, which they called the Cape Colony, but South Africa's interior was very similar to the American frontier.

There was the well-organized, numerous, and often bellicose Zulus, who lived in the eastern portion of South Africa in a province that became known as Natal. The Zulus were an African Bantu tribe that had migrated to the region from central Africa hundreds of years earlier, defeating other tribes as they made their journey south and adopting the lifestyle of cattle herding in the process.

Between the Zulus and the British were numerous African tribes that were less organized, or a threat to the British, but there was also a sizable number of people known as Boers or Afrikaners.

The Boers (Dutch for "farmer") were primarily Dutch Calvinist (remember them?) immigrants who wanted land of their own to farm, far away from the Zulus *and* British. After the Boers clashed with the Zulus and came to a basic understanding with them, they moved to South Africa's interior and developed a unique culture.

The form of Dutch that the Boers spoke diverged so much from the original Dutch that it became a new language known as Afrikaans and their culture was based very much on the idea of Calvinist predestination and often hostility toward the British.

I guess a good way to look at the Boers is as militant Pilgrims but with better guns!

The British left them alone for the most part, and eventually the semi-autonomous Boer states of Transvaal and the Orange Free State were formed.

Everything seemed fine between the British, Zulus, and Boers (they didn't necessarily like each other, but they stayed out of each other's way) until diamonds were discovered in the lower Vaal River valley, Orange Free State in 1867.

The discovery brought thousands of new immigrants into the Orange Free State, much to the chagrin of the Boers.

Even more change came to the region when diamonds were discovered outside of the town of Kimberley in 1871. The result was a mad rush to extract all the diamonds from the mine that changed the face of South Africa, politically, socially, and physically, and left ripple effects that are still felt today.

The land where the Kimberley mine was located was owned by brothers Johannes and Diederik De Beer. The De Beer brothers found themselves in an unfortunate position, though, as they were heavily pressured by the British government to sell their land. So, they did, to future Cape Colony Prime Minister Cecil Rhodes.

Rhodes then received funding from Nathan Rothschild of *the* Rothschild family, and for whatever reason, they decided to name the company "De Beers" because they probably thought the Dutch name would go over better with the locals. The reality is that the De Beer brothers had nothing to do with the company after they sold it to Rhodes.

The Kimberley mine became known as the "Big Hole" because, well, today it's a big hole partially filled with water. From its existence to its depletion in 1914, more than 6,000 pounds of diamonds or 13,600,000 carats were excavated from the mine.

But that wasn't the only thing the Kimberley mine dug up in South Africa.

With the influx of new money and people, tensions between the Boers, British, and Zulus raised to a fever pitch by the late 1870s.

As the British tried to take complete control over the Orange Free State and Transvaal, the Zulus attacked British outposts in 1879, starting the Anglo-Zulu War. Although the Zulus lost, the Boers decided they would give it a try in their own lands.

The First Anglo-Boer War was fought from December 16, 1880, to March 23, 1881, with the Boers gaining their independence. The British kept Kimberley and the diamond mine, but this story was far from over.

More gold and diamonds were found near Pretoria, the capital of the South African Republic (formerly Transvaal) in the 1890s, which prompted Rhodes to organize an attempted coup of that country's government.

When that failed, Britain invaded the Boer republics on October 11, 1899, starting the Second Boer War.

The Boers used guerilla tactics against the British, picking up a thing or two from the Zulus, but in the end, the British decided that the gold and diamonds were just too valuable. They could afford to lose 22,000 of their men, and when that didn't work, they weren't afraid to become even more brutal.

The British finally won the Second Boer War when they put all the Boer fighters' wives and children in concentration camps. Yes, the first modern concentration camps were a British invention that were built and administered in South Africa.

The concentration camps worked; sort of. The British won the war, got their diamonds and gold, and made South Africa a colony.

But South Africa was never *really* a British colony. South Africans pursued their own development, including the apartheid racial policy, which the British generally opposed.

The discovery of the diamonds in Kimberley eventually helped make South Africa the wealthiest and most developed country in Africa, but it came at great costs. The people of the country were, and still are in many ways, deeply divided by race and ethnicity - Black, White, and Asian; British, Boer/Afrikaner, and Zulu - with all sides claiming a heritage that was tough, to begin with, but only made bloodier once diamonds were discovered in Kimberley in 1871.

"MR. WATSON—COME HERE—
I WANT TO SEE YOU."

If you love your smartphone, and chances are more than a few of you reading this do, then the date March 12, 1876, should be important to you. It was on that date that Scottish born, American, and Canadian, inventor Alexander Graham Bell uttered the famous words, "Mr. Watson - come here - I want to see you," to his assistant Thomas Watson, on the world's first functional telephone.

It was the culmination of years of experiments by Bell and Watson, who was a successful engineer in his own right, in a Boston, Massachusetts laboratory. Actually, for Bell, his journey to create the phone began years earlier in his native Scotland. Born in 1847 to a middle-class family, Bell's father, Alexander Melville Bell, was a professor of phonetics, so learning was constantly nurtured in the Bell home.

Young Alexander constantly tinkered, inventing the de-husking machine at the age of 12 before moving into the field that made him famous. It was also when Alexander Graham was 12 that his mother, Eliza, began losing her hearing. Alexander then dedicated most of his research to audio science and helping the hearing impaired.

The next major event in Bell's life, and the one that led to his monumental invention, was his family's move to Canada in 1870. The openness and clean air of Canada helped to reinvigorate Bell's research and it also put him physically close to the United States. He later moved to Boston where he began working with the deaf as well as conducting his own experiments on the telephone with Thomas Watson.

Bell and Watson's invention was ultimately the winning entry in an unofficial race to invent the first working telephone.

Inventor Elisha Gray actually filled his telephone patent first, but it was Bell who was remembered as the inventor of the phone and therefore the person who had the greatest impact. A major reason for that was because Bell was as successful a businessman as he was an inventor. As soon as it was proved that his phone worked, Bell began doing public demonstrations and inviting investors into his company.

Gray and other notable inventors, such as Thomas Edison, would later improve upon Bell's invention with microphones and other innovations, as is often the case when a notable invention is made.

Bell's invention was great, but it needed something more to make it practical. The early phone was only useful for person-to-person calls, and each party had to be ready for the call.

So, in 1877, just months after Bell made his historic first call, Hungarian engineer Tivadar Puskás invented the first telephone exchange and followed that up with the invention of the multiplex switchboard in 1887.

This basic technology was what was used for the next 100 plus years. Human operators were all but replaced by automatic switchboards in the late 1960s, but the concept was more or less the same.

And it all began on that cold night in Boston in 1876.

SO SIMPLE YET
SO IMPORTANT

Sticking with the theme of inventions that proved to be earthshattering events, let's take a look at one of the most seemingly simple inventions in human history - the incandescent light bulb. Before 1880, the method of producing artificial light hadn't changed much from the Paleolithic Period. In fact, they were making light more or less the same way during the Civil War as the cave men did thousands of years earlier.

Sure, people were using oil lamps in the 1800s instead of torches, but the technology was essentially the same. You simply find some oil or another mineral or substance that burns, light it, and then you have light.

Nothing complicated about it.

But as simple as getting light from burning things is, it obviously has its limitations. You're dependent on materials that are flammable, which aren't always available.

And they're not always safe.

Not to mention using a flame for light isn't the most practical source of artificial light. Turning the flame on and off isn't an option in many cases.

But by the mid-1800s, a number of things had changed. We already saw how Benjamin Franklin's experiment with lightning led to more advances in electricity, so let's take a look at the next great leap forward.

Thomas Alva Edison is rightfully remembered as one of America's greatest inventors and scientists, like Alexander Graham Bell, and also like Bell, he was a great businessman who knew how to sell his ideas. Born in 1847 in Milan, Ohio, Edison lost most of his hearing as a child, which made things difficult for him, but it didn't prevent him from pursuing his love of science and technology.

Edison worked as a telegraph operator while he was in his 20s, which gave him the chance to work hands-on with technology and to pursue some of his own ideas in his spare time. Throughout his life, Edison would file over 1,000 patents, including the phonograph, a moving-picture projector, alkaline storage batteries, and an electric railroad train.

The invention of the phonograph in 1877 was Edison's first big breakthrough, which brought in enough money for him to keep funding his lab in Menlo Park, New Jersey for even bigger experiments.

Like the invention of the incandescent light bulb.

The idea of the incandescent light bulb is simple enough: it requires a filament enclosed in a vacuum glass bulb and an inert gas. The trick is getting the electricity there to light the filament. Not long after Ben Franklin did his kite experiment, inventors began trying to create such a light bulb.

But all soon found out that making an incandescent light bulb wasn't as easy as it seemed.

A few things combined in the mid-1800s to move things forward and make the light bulb a reality. The Industrial Revolution had come full force to the United States by that time, and when combined with the young country's growing population, there were plenty of people who wanted to experiment.

The US also became a haven for European immigrants at that time who were escaping political persecution (remember the 1848 revolutions?) or to take part in America's sense of optimism and its entrepreneurial spirit and love of free enterprise. One such immigrant was a Russian inventor named Alexander Lodygin.

Lodygin fled to the United States in 1884 to escape political persecution, but not before getting a Russian patent for the incandescent light bulb he invented in 1872.

A British inventor named Joseph Swan also received a patent for an incandescent light bulb in 1880, but it was Edison's light bulb that changed history.

On November 4, 1879, Edison filed a patent for his version of the incandescent light bulb, which featured a carbon filament. The patent was granted in January 1880, almost instantly changing the world. Although there were other brilliant inventors who developed versions of the light bulb, few were brilliant inventors *and* brilliant businessmen.

Just before his groundbreaking invention, Edison formed the Edison Electric Light Company in 1878 with the financial backing of *the* J.P. Morgan as well as a number of other notable tycoons from the era. Edison was finally able to bring his vision to the world, beginning with the United States.

He made further improvements on the incandescent light bulb, such as using a carbonized bamboo filament, which would allow the lightbulbs to last hundreds or even thousands of hours. Once that light bulb was perfected, and he had financial backing, Edison proceeded with his next step of making the "consumption" of electricity practical.

Only two years after he received his light bulb patent, Edison devised the country's first electrical power plant in New York City in 1883. Although it brought power to only 100 customers in the city it eventually grew to service over 500 customers, it was the beginning of something big.

Once Edison invented the light bulb, he made sure that the world would never go back to using torches.

REMEMBER THE MAINE

In the decades after the Civil War, the United States sank into a sort of geopolitical complacency. The American government and people focused on their domestic issues and the economy more than foreign affairs. Sure, not everything was great for everyone in the US, but things were more or less peaceful at home and abroad.

But by the late 1800s, the Americans began emerging from their cocoon, beginning with their involvement in Asia that we talked about earlier.

American presidents from both major parties wanted to protect American interests in the Pacific and Asia, which they considered their "backyard" in some ways. So, as the European powers began staking their claims in treaty ports, the Americans thought they should get involved as well.

But the Americans' true backyard was Latin America.

During President McKinley's one term as US President (1897-1901) - we'll get to that in a little bit - the US became more territorial, enforcing the Monroe Doctrine. The Monroe Doctrine was an idea, never a law or official decree, first advanced by the fifth American president, James Monroe, in 1823. The doctrine basically stated that the US wouldn't let European powers recolonize the Americas, but there was plenty of gray area concerning the colonies those powers still had there.

For the decades after the Monroe Doctrine's promulgation, it was never an issue. Spain had the most colonies in the Americas, and they had lost most of them in the early 1800s and never tried to regain any. But in the late 1800s, it still had a few colonies in the region, like Cuba and Puerto Rico, that ultimately posed more problems than benefits for Spain.

The Cuban people gradually grew tired of their Spanish overlords. They may have spoken the same language, but by the late 1800s, Cuba was very different from Spain. The cultures developed differently and in terms of geography, Cuba was much closer to the United States. Both of these factors led to a Cuban independence movement starting, which in turn led to the Cuban War of Independence.

Many Americans were on-board with the Cubans for a number of reasons.

Many average Americans genuinely believed the Cubans should have their own government and saw their independence struggle as like the American Revolution. They simply believed that any people should have the right to choose their own government. And just as America's Founding Fathers fought against a tyrannical government in Europe, Cuba's freedom fighters were doing the same.

But there were also many Americans who supported Cuban independence due to ulterior motives.

Some in the military and government saw the opportunity to create an American Empire using the European model.

There were also wealthy Americans who wanted to get into the sugar and rum trades.

And finally, the newspapers of the era saw the conflict as a way to sell papers. The big newspaper owners, editors, and writers probably didn't care about Cuba one way or the other, but they knew that printing stories about Spanish atrocities on Cubans, real or imagined, was a good way to sell papers.

This was the start of the era of "yellow journalism."

So, all of this came together on the night of February 15, 1898, when the US Navy ship the USS *Maine* was sunk as a result of an onboard explosion in the harbor of Havana, Cuba.

The consequences of the sinking of the *Maine* were immediate and felt throughout the world. The ship, which was in Havana harbor to "protect US interests," was destroyed and 260 of its crewmen lost their lives. Although it was never determined what caused the explosion, and the initial investigation proceeded with some caution, hotheads in the government and the yellow press quickly pointed the finger at Spain.

Few stopped to ask how the *Maine's* destruction would benefit Spain, or how they got on board to set off the explosion. President McKinley initially favored restraint, but Assistant Secretary of the Navy, Theodore "Teddy" Roosevelt, and others convinced the president that a blockade of Cuba was the only option.

In retrospect, the *Maine's* explosion could have been caused by a number of things, most of which would have been accidental or due to the ship's obsolescence. None of that mattered at the time, though, when there were so many people in the US interested in war.

Spain and the US declared war on each other, and from April 21 to August 13, 1898, fought what became known as the Spanish-American War.

The war had only a few minor battles and less than 1,000 men were killed on both sides, but the repercussions were massive.

When the two countries signed a peace treaty in Paris, the world's geopolitical scene changed in an instant. Spain's long descent from *the* world's superpower in the 1500s to an imperial also-ran was complete. It continued to hold a few colonies but nowhere near what it did during its heyday.

On the other hand, the United States acquired Puerto Rico, Guam, and the Philippines, instantly becoming a colonial power. The US then engaged in several military operations throughout Latin America, overtly in the early 1900s and more covertly after World War II.

Puerto Rico and Guam are still American territories and US bases, and Americans dot the now independent Philippines.

The role of the press and its ability to influence people with "fake news" (yellow journalism was just the term for fake news of that era) became a standard after the destruction of the *Maine*. Today, some would say that the press hasn't changed a bit since 1898 and has only gotten worse, while others say that most major press outlets are objective.

I guess that's for you to decide.

Teddy Roosevelt became a national figure after the explosion of the *Maine*, resigning his position as Assistant Secretary of the Navy to organize and help lead the Rough Riders unit of the Army. Although Roosevelt was somewhat of a legend in his own mind in many ways, he did lead his men at the Battle of San Juan Hill where he famously urged his men to charge, shouting "Remember the Maine!"

Roosevelt parlayed his rise in stature to win the New York governor's office in 1898 before moving on to accept the vice presidency under President McKinley during his second term.

But after just a few short months into his second term, McKinley was assassinated by an anarchist, making Roosevelt the president. Of course, TR, as Roosevelt was also known, went on to become one of the most influential American presidents, responsible for breaking up corporate monopolies and having the Panama Canal constructed.

After serving nearly two terms as president, Roosevelt later left the Republican Party and ran as an independent in 1912, splitting the vote and, some say, handing the election to Democrat Woodrow Wilson.

It's crazy to think that all of that happened due to the bombing of the *Maine* by someone, or something, that remains a mystery to this day.

REACHING FOR THE SKIES

You probably get the idea that by the late 1800s, all the hard work and sacrifices of the Renaissance, Enlightenment, and Industrial Revolution began paying off with incredible dividends. Men like Copernicus, Newton, and Franklin laid the groundwork for later inventors such as Bell and Edison to make the next major leaps forward.

And by the early 1900s, humans were taking that accumulated knowledge and going beyond the Earth's surface.

Flight was something humans had dreamed of since the dawn of human civilization. The ancient Greeks told the story of how a man named Icarus made wings from wax and was able to fly with them but crashed to the Earth when he flew too close to the sun.

Although Icarus was a myth, humans knew from an early point that defying gravity was a *possibility*.

Medieval Chinese scientists theorized about how flight could be possible, and Leonardo Da Vinci did the same during the Renaissance, but flight remained theoretical until the late 1700s when hot air balloons began taking people into the air.

Yes, hot air balloons do fly, but they aren't airplanes or "heavier than air machines," as planes are technically called.

The first heavier than air flight would be the next great leap forward in human civilization, but like some of the other inventions and discoveries we've looked at, it was less the result of a giant leap and more so the culmination of several baby steps.

Thanks to the many advances of the Renaissance, Enlightenment, and the Industrial Age, British scholar and engineer George Cayley began developing a genuine, scientific theory of the possibility of a heavier than air, fixed-wing aircraft flying. At some time before 1849, he designed and built a biplane in which an unknown ten-year-old boy flew. Using the principles of previous ancient, medieval, and modern scholars, Cayley published his ideas in 1852. Although Cayley never put his theories into practice, two brothers who owned a bicycle shop in Dayton, Ohio took a keen interest.

In 1903, Wilbur and Orville Wright were successful bicycle manufacturers and shop owners. You may find this hard to believe, but in the late 1890s, the pedal bike/bicycle was a fairly new invention that had become quite popular, although people didn't quite know if it was for recreation or transportation. The bicycles were quite different-looking to what we know as bikes of today, were difficult to control, and were fairly expensive, so they were often as much a show of status as they were a vehicle for getting around town.

Although most people didn't really know what to make of early bikes, they continued to sell well, especially as their designs improved and they became easier to ride.

The Wright brothers, who were self-educated geniuses, saw the potential of both uses and began producing and marketing their own bikes in 1896. The business helped the Wright brothers become financially secure and allowed them to pursue their true dream, and the dream of human civilization, flight.

It was no easy journey for the Wright brothers, and when it comes to something so incredible as the first flight, why would it have been?

The Wright brothers continued to work at their bike shop and in their free time, they began assembling their new, one-of-a-kind plane, which they called the *Wright Flyer*.

The *Wright Flyer* wasn't much of a plane by modern standards - or actually it was, in some ways. It only had a single, four-piston engine that was supposed to propel a double-wing craft that weighed 605 pounds!

The engine was the last piece of the puzzle the Wright brothers had to consider. They had done several "gliding" flights of their plane without the engine, so when they finally added the engine and attempted their first flight on December 14, 1903.

The flight was *nearly* successful, but close doesn't cut it in flight, so the Wright brothers had to try again.

On December 17, 1903, each of the Wright brothers successfully took turns flying the one-man plane on a desolate sand dune near Kitty Hawk, North Carolina, becoming the first people to fly in a heavier than air, fixed-wing craft. Orville was technically the first to accomplish the feat, flying for about 120 feet for 12 seconds, only about ten feet of the ground.

So, what impact did the Wright brothers' flight have on the world?

The answer to this question is obvious, but I think it's even more incredible when you put it into perspective. The first hot air balloon flight was in 1782, 121 years before the Wright brothers essentially invented the airplane. That's quite a long time when you consider that *after* the Wright brothers' invention, airplanes were being used in World War II just over ten years later.

Charles Lindbergh made the first non-stop trans-Atlantic flight in 1927 and by the 1940s, the first jet airplanes were being used by Germany in World War II.

So, it took 121 years to go from a hot air balloon to an airplane, but after the Wright brothers, it only took 40 years to get jets.

Now that's pretty incredible when you think about it!

RUSSIA WAS SUPPOSED TO WIN THAT WAR

If you've been reading this encyclopedia from the beginning, then you've probably noticed that some of the important events we covered earlier led to some even bigger events later. Our next key event is a perfect example of that, as it was the result of things set in motion after the Sengoku in Japan and the Opium Wars in China.

If you'll remember, one of the major impacts of the Opium Wars was that it opened China to the West with the treaty ports. Great Britain, France, Germany, and even the United States got involved in exploiting the treaty ports, but so too did Russia and Japan.

Japan's case was certainly interesting.

Japan was the only Asian nation in the club of foreign countries that were essentially colonizing China via the treaty ports. The Japanese embarked on an incredible program of modernization in the mid- to late-1800s to build a modern navy and army that could compete with any of the Western powers. Then, after building their military, they quickly went out to build their empire.

The Japanese focused most of their imperial attention on Manchuria and Korea, which caused them to rub soldiers with the Russians.

Russia, too, was an interesting case in the treaty port and Asian colonization situation.

Russia's history and culture have always been tied to the West *and* East. Most of the Russian people are European, they speak a European language, and they are predominantly Orthodox Christians. Historically, Russia has also been closely tied to other Eastern European countries, particularly Greece. When Rome collapsed and its money and power moved to Constantinople, the Greek city became known as the "Second Rome."

And when Constantinople fell to the Ottoman Turks in 1453, Moscow, Russia became the heart of Orthodox Christianity in Europe and become known as the "Third Rome." Or at least that is what Russians called it.

But to the people of Western Europe, Russia remained a backward, exotic country that was as Asian as it was European.

And that perception was based on some truth. The Russian people have historically dressed differently from other Europeans and even groomed themselves differently. The beard, which was always more popular in central Asian and Islamic countries than Europe, was also popular with Russian men. A lot of traditional Russian clothing, some foods, and elements of their folk culture were also influenced as much by Asia as by Europe.

The Russian royals, who were connected by marriage to the royals of numerous European countries, West and East, were keenly aware of this and constantly did what they could to appear to be "one of the boys." Peter the Great even outlawed

Russian nobles from wearing beards! But another more impactful way the Russians tried to gain the respect of their European cousins was by expanding their borders in the late 1800s to become an imperial power.

Or a 'sort' of imperial power.

Russia was definitely moving east and had claimed land all the way to the west coast of what would become the United States in the early 1800s. They eventually gave those far-flung lands up and concentrated on their land in Eurasia to the Pacific. But there was one big problem with all that land.

It was too cold!

Some people like cold weather and can even thrive in it, but it's tough to have a world-class navy when your major ports are frozen part of the year. The Russian port of Vladivostok became a happening place and the site of the Russian Navy's Pacific fleet, but it was frozen during the winter months.

So, the Russians had to look just a bit farther south for a year-round, warm water port.

Port Arthur in the Liaoning province of China appeared to be the perfect place. The only problem was the Japanese conquered it in 1894. Through some diplomatic maneuvering, though, the Russians were able to get France and Germany on board with a plan whereby they threatened Japan with war if Japan didn't give up Port Arthur.

The Russians then quickly moved in and commenced building a railroad from Port Arthur to the Russian city of Harbin.

Here's where things get interesting, and the Russians' arrogance got the best of them. Ironically, the Russians made the same mistake toward the Japanese that Napoleon did toward them nearly 100 years earlier - they underestimated their opponent.

The Japanese entered negotiations with the Russians over possessions in China and Korea from a position of relative strength, although they didn't show their hand, nor did they underestimate the Russians. The Japanese had built a state-of-the-art modern naval fleet in the late 1800s. Most importantly, they were close to where all the action was so they could transport soldiers quickly to the battlefields if war broke out.

They offered the Russians all of Manchuria in return for northern Korea.

Russian Tsar Nicholas II was perhaps a bit influenced by the anti-Asian propaganda of the day and possibly goaded by the other European powers who may have benefitted from conflict. Nicholas refused to offer any serious compromises, so the Japanese attacked Port Arthur on February 8, 1904, starting the Russo-Japanese War.

Many in the West, owing to racial sentiments of the era, thought the war would be over quickly. It was believed the White Russians would simply sail to Asia, slap the little Japanese around a bit, and then take what they wanted.

But oh, how wrong they were.

The Russian military was plagued by incompetent leadership, logistical problems (getting troops from European Russia to Asia was a problem), and low morale among its troops. On the other hand, the Japanese military was a well-disciplined force that used modern equipment and didn't have to travel far to the battlefields in Korea and China.

The size of the armies was comparable, with over one million total on each side, and the Japanese suffered more casualties, but it was a fight the Russians didn't expect.

The Japanese Navy dominated the Russian Navy, sinking eight Russian battleships and capturing two, while only losing two of their battleships. Japanese naval dominance ensured that the Russians would find it nearly impossible to bring reinforcements by ship from European Russia in the later stages of the war.

The fighting on land was extremely brutal and although the Russians did better there, they still came out the losers. The Battle of Mukden, which was fought in Manchuria from February 20 to March 10, 1905, proved to be the last significant battle in the Russo-Japanese War. The Japanese won the battle, giving them an easier march to Harbin, forcing the Russians to agree to a pro-Japanese peace treaty.

No one would have thought that the Japanese could have so decisively defeated the Russians - well, actually Adolf Hitler did, as he related in *Mein Kampf* how he rooted for his future allies against his hated Russian enemies - but they should have thought more about it if they looked at the big picture.

The Russo-Japanese War was in many ways a prelude to World War I. Many of the tactics and weaponry the Japanese successfully used against the Russians were used on the battlefields of the Great War.

For the Japanese, the Russo-Japanese War cemented their place as a modern imperial power. The Treaty of Portsmouth, which the Americans hosted and moderated, gave the Japanese Port Arthur and other ports as well as all of Korea.

Japan would ride the imperial wave of good fortune into World War II, and it would play a major role in their joining the Axis Powers.

What about Russia?

Well, Russia's loss in the Russo-Japanese War was devastating, to say the least. With economic and social problems already rampant in Russia, the loss on the battlefield triggered an attempted revolution that was led by socialist and communist groups. Although the Tsar was able to suppress the revolution, it was not totally extinguished.

The communists wouldn't have to wait long for another chance.

HENRY FORD KNEW THE MODEL T WOULD CHANGE THE WORLD

Henry Ford was a true American original. Born during the Civil War in 1863 outside Dearborn, Michigan, Ford rode the great wave of American innovation along with Bell, Edison, and the Wright brothers. Many could argue that Ford's contribution to important events that shaped modern world history was even greater than the first phone call or first flight, although it's often misunderstood.

You may think that Henry Ford invented the automobile, but you'd be wrong. That honor is generally given to German Carl (often Karl) Benz, who in 1885 invented what would be the first true automobile. Benz, of course, became well-known for starting that auto company that would later make the luxury car, Mercedes-Benz.

So, why do so many people think Ford invented the automobile and what event was he part of that had such a great impact on history?

Well, the answer to the first part is that Ford *was* automobiles in the United States in the late 1800s and early 1900s.

Ford's journey to greatness began with relatively humble origins in Michigan, where he discovered his aptitude for mechanics by fixing his friends and family members' watches when he was 15. He progressed from watches to steam engines and just about anything mechanical he could get his hands on, which he did without any formal education.

Young Ford's reputation as an engineer eventually preceded him, helping him land a job at the Edison Illuminating Company, where he was eventually able to meet his hero, Thomas Edison, in 1896. But as much as Ford respected Edison, his true interest was in the emerging science of automotive engineering.

Like Bell, Edison, and the Wright brothers, Ford was also a keen businessman who was always looking to capitalize on his scientific advances, although he wasn't always so successful. Ford's first attempt at starting a motor company failed in 1901, but when he tried again with the Ford Motor Company in 1903, it proved to be a success.

The creation of the Ford Motor Company paved the way for Ford to create an event that truly changed the world.

On October 1, 1908, the way the world did business immediately changed when the first Model T car was sold. What makes that such an incredible moment isn't necessarily the car itself, although it was quite reliable and of a higher quality than most cars of the era, but *how* it was made.

The Model T was initially assembled like most other automobiles at the time, by hand, making one complete car at a time. Only 11 Model Ts were made during the first month of production, causing Ford to give the production a second look. He knew that things could be done faster, and more efficiently; after all, the US was post-Industrial Revolution by that point, so there wasn't any reason why the burgeoning automotive industry shouldn't take advantage of the technology.

So, Ford introduced one genius, yet simple idea to make cars faster - the assembly line.

As with the car, Ford didn't invent the assembly line, but he was the first person to put the two together, leaving many people later scratching their heads, saying "why didn't I think of that?"

The use of the assembly immediately paid off for Ford, with 12,000 Model Ts being produced in 1910, far outproducing the competition. By 1914, it only took 93 minutes to produce one Model T. The numbers were incredible for the time, with the Ford Motor Company producing more than 15 million Model Ts from 1908 to 1927, averaging about 10,000 a day in the 1920s.

The impact of that first Model T coming off the assembly line in 1908 was immediately felt across the United States. Thanks to its high production, the Model T was sold at prices that middle- and working-class Americans could afford. No longer were cars the property of just the rich; all Americans could own one.

And as Americans bought Model Ts, the face of America changed in more than one way.

In 1913, the Lincoln Highway was completed, becoming the first trans-American highway. Soon other roads would follow and before long, the first freeways and interstates highways began cobwebbing across America.

The invention of the Model T also had some social implications in the US.

It's no coincidence that the availability and the popularity of the Model T coincided with the Roaring '20s, when young people questioned social norms, some of them sexual, and often in the back seat of a Model T!

But the revolution of the Model T wasn't just limited to cars, the Ford Motor Company, or even the United States. The assembly line became the standard method of mass production in all industrialized nations in the 20th century. And as soulless as the assembly line may seem to many of us today, it helped propel the world through the Industrial Age into the Computer/Internet Age that we now live in.

Few people thought that that Model T would have such an impact on the world when it first rolled out on October 1, 1908, but as a true visionary, Henry Ford would have told you so if you'd asked him.

CAN YOU IMAGINE *NOT* HAVING ANTIBIOTICS?

For the vast majority of human history, people didn't know precisely what caused them to get sick. Today, we know that viruses and bacteria cause most illnesses, but to put things into their proper historical perspective, it's important to point out that viruses weren't discovered until 1898.

As for bacteria…

Well, the idea of bacteria, including what they are and how they are spread, has been closely tied to virology, although they are two different things. That was probably part of the confusion throughout the centuries. Contrary to popular opinion, most people in ancient and medieval societies knew that dirt and uncleanliness could be bad for health and could get you sick, although there were often religious tones to any explanation.

Maybe plagues are caused by bad food?

Could sickness possibly come in the air?

Does sexual intercourse bring diseases or relieve one from it?

These were all ideas that were bandied about to explain bacteria and viruses, but it wasn't until the early 1800s that "germ theory" finally started to make headway in academia and the medical profession. Scientists discovered what bacteria was and how it was transmitted to humans in many cases, but they hadn't yet discovered how to kill harmful bacteria that enters the human body.

German scientist Paul Ehrlich began experimenting with antibacterial medicines to varying degrees of success in the late 1800s. When he discovered that certain dyes affected human and animal cells, he reasoned that 'specific' medicines could be made to attack bacteria in human, or animal, bodies.

So, with Japanese scientist Sahachiro Hata, Ehrlich began creating a number of compounds to develop the first true antibiotic. In 1909, the pair made it to compound number 606 when they made an incredible breakthrough.

Now, here's where our next important historical event becomes a little…um, icky, I guess you could say.

Compound 606, or Salvarsan, was an incredible medical advance because it was the first true antibiotic medicine, but what makes this so interesting is that when Ehrlich and Hata announced the discovery to the world in 1910, the medicine was intended to treat syphilis.

As uncomfortable as talk of the sexually transmitted disease syphilis may make all of us, it was a scourge that caused problems for centuries or longer. It's believed that syphilis was a New World disease that sailors and explorers brought back to Europe after they sewed their oats in the Americas.

From there, syphilis spread wherever there was a desire for sex and men willing to pay for it. In other words, it spread very quickly!

Beyond causing problems down below, syphilis can create issues up above as well in the form of mental problems, painful rashes throughout the body, and eventually death. Even worse, syphilis can be passed from mother to child, giving the innocent victims of congenital syphilis grotesque features.

So, Ehrlich and Hata's discovery was a pretty big deal. Syphilis immediately went from being an incurable curse on the land to something that was quite controllable. But the long-term ramifications of the pair's discovery were even greater.

Research into antibiotic medicine gained steam after 1910 and for the next 20 years, new discoveries were made around the world, the most important of which was the Scottish scientist Alexander Fleming's 1928 discovery of penicillin.

Penicillin went on to become the gold standard of antibiotic medication and the technology behind its discovery formed the basis of all subsequent antibiotics. Fleming's discovery wouldn't have been possible without Ehrlich and Hata's discovery first, though.

Thanks to Ehrlich and Hata, we often only have to take a shot or some pills to defeat what once would have been life-threatening infections. I can't imagine living in a world without antibiotic medicine, so for that reason, I think their discovery was one of the greatest achievements in modern history.

A WRONG TURN STARTED
A WORLD WAR

On June 28, 1914, the world changed in an instant. It was on that day that the Archduke (heir apparent) of the Austro-Hungarian Empire, Franz Ferdinand, and his wife Sophie, the Duchess of Hohenberg, were assassinated by a team of Serbian nationalists. Regicide is always a major event and this one proved to be the match to light the powder keg that Europe was sitting on at the time.

But the assassination wouldn't have happened if not for a simple mistake, or fate, whichever one you want to believe.

Yes, the Archduke and his wife were the targets of a well-conceived plot by a group of motivated, well-armed, and fairly well-trained men. And they were also the target of previous assassination plots. However, that fact combined with two failures by the assassins on the morning of June 28 seemed to indicate that fate was actually on the side of the archduke.

But then his driver made a wrong turn, and the rest is as they say, history.

So, how did the assassination take place, how did it almost not happen, and what were its implications, great and small?

Once again, this major event is connected to some major events we looked at earlier in this book. In particular, the events of 1848, when revolutions were rolling across Europe. If you remember, nationalist revolutions were put down in the Austrian Empire, with the authorities' giving concessions to the Hungarians.

But not the Slavs.

Never confuse Hungarians with Slavs or vice versa. They may live in the same geographic area, but their languages are very different, and they have different histories. So, the Hungarians were more or less satisfied when the Austrian Empire became the Austro-Hungarian Empire in 1867, but the Czechs, Slovenes, Serbs, Croats and Bosniaks remained minor players in this multi-ethnic empire. The area of southeast Europe where most of these groups lived, known as the "Balkans," remained a backwater, but it was a backwater with plenty of people who had a lot of reasons to be angry.

And as the Ottoman Empire rapidly declined throughout the 1800s into the 1900s, becoming the "sick man of Europe," Austria-Hungary was there to gobble up many of its former European possessions.

That's how Austria-Hungary took possession of Bosnia and Herzegovina in 1908.

The people of Bosnia and Herzegovina found themselves in essentially the same position they were in under Ottoman rule, with foreign rulers telling them what to do, although a combination of religious dynamics and current events meant that things would turn out differently.

The Ottomans were Muslims and were opposed by the Orthodox Christian Serbs and the Roman Catholic Croats, but sometimes supported by the Muslim Bosniaks. When the Austrian-Hungarians, who were Roman Catholics, became the new rulers the dynamics changed again. The Bosniaks no longer had religious support from above, the Croats had a religiously friendly power on the throne, and the Serbs were still more or less out of luck.

Add to this the fervor of nationalism (remember that?) that had been sweeping over Europe since the mid-19th century, and you had a recipe disaster.

Serbian nationalists began organizing, both in secret and openly. Among those who organized in secret was a group known as the Black Hand, which advocated violence and terrorism to push Austria-Hungary out of Bosnia so that Bosnian Serbs could unite Bosnia and Serbia.

An important "above ground" Serbian nationalist group in Bosnia at the time was called the Young Bosnia movement. The Young Bosnians primarily engaged in street protests, but by 1914, many of them were moving into violence and became involved with the Black Hand.

This is when a Serbian nationalist named Gavrilo Princip began putting together an assassination team that wouldn't fail.

Through his connections in Young Bosnia and the Black Hand, Princip was able to gather money, guns, bombs, and cars that would be needed to transport and house his team, as well the means to carry out the killings in the city of Sarajevo. The hit team included Princip and five other men, although many others helped with the logistics.

When the team learned that the Archduke and his wife would be visiting Sarajevo on June 28, it seemed too good to be true.

Moreover, the date chosen for this imperial visit and Hapsburg show of force was June 28, a black date in Serbian history: it was the anniversary of the Turkish victory over Serbia at the Battle of Kosovo in 1389.

It was also the date of the Feast of St. Vitus, which for Serbian Orthodox Christians is a celebration of the Battle of Kosovo in 1389. In that battle, the Serbs fought the Ottomans to a draw, but the Ottoman sultan, Murad I, was stabbed to death in his tent by a Serbian knight named Milos Obilic.

Or, at least, that's what the Serbs believed and continued to believe into the 20th century. As you know from reading this book, history is powerful, and sometimes even more powerful than the history itself is the perception or narrative of history. Those who control a historical narrative have the ability to influence current events and the future.

So, for the Serbs, Milos Obilic became a hero, no matter what opposing opinions may have said about the veracity of why he committed the assassination, or if he even did it. And Princip was bound and determined to be the modern era's Obilic.

The conspirators learned the route of the archduke's motorcade and placed assassins at key spots to ensure that if one missed, another would be able to carry out the act. But once the royal motorcade came strolling through the streets of Sarajevo, it was amateur hour for the assassins.

The royal motorcade was to originally have six cars, but a car full of security officers was left behind, leaving the archduke with a more local, less trained security detail.

The royals first visited a military barracks at 10 a.m. before driving through the central city on their way to city hall. The motorcade passed by two would-be assassins who were armed with guns and bombs, but they lost their nerves.

Not exactly Milos Obilic, but there were still four more assassins waiting.

Assassin number three kept his nerve, though, and got close enough to throw a bomb at the archduke's car, but it bounced off and exploded under one of the other cars in the motorcade.

The archduke then went to the city hall where he bravely gave a speech before announcing that he'd make another stop to visit those in the hospital who were injured in the bombing.

You can say what you want about Ferdinand being spoiled and born with a silver spoon. Or you can even say that he didn't care about some of his subjects. However, you definitely can't say the man was a coward! Most modern leaders wouldn't be seen for weeks after a legitimate assassination attempt like the one Ferdinand experienced, but Ferdinand was clearly cut from the cloth of an earlier time.

He may have been brave, but maybe not very wise.

So, like a general leading his troops, Ferdinand led the royal procession from the city hall to the hospital…and to his destiny.

As the procession made its way down Appel Quay, the Archduke's driver made a right turn at the Latin Bridge, onto Franz Joseph Street, instead of a left turn. When the archduke's driver realized he'd made a wrong turn, he hit the brakes to back up, but by chance, Princip was there waiting. Princip rushed the car, jumped on its running board, and fired a shot from his pistol into the archduke and another into the duchess.

He was caught before he could put a third bullet into his own head.

Sophie died almost instantly while Ferdinand was dead on arrival at the hospital.

The assassinations immediately thrust Bosnia into ethnic turmoil among Serbs, Croats, and Bosniaks, which quickly spread throughout Europe. Although there was no evidence the Serbian government was involved in the assassination, Austria-Hungary demanded that it allowed Austrian police into its borders to arrest Serbian nationalists.

The tiny Slavic country tried to resist diplomatically, which only seemed to anger the Austro-Hungarians more.

Finally, when Serbia didn't fully capitulate, Austria-Hungary declared war on it on July 28, 1914. The pre-war alliance system was then activated, with Russia declaring war on Austria-Hungary, Germany declaring war on Russia, France, and Belgium, and then Britain declaring war on Germany.

Although many factors led up to World War I, including nationalism, colonialism, and the alliance system, a wrong turn is what set it all off.

COMMUNIST REVOLUTION AND REGICIDE IN RUSSIA

Let's keep with the idea of regicide as we move on in our book. Regicide is the act of killing a king, queen, emperor, shah, sultan, or any other ruler who gained power through a royal line/dynasty. It's that last point that separates a regicide from a garden variety assassination. In the case of Ferdinand's assassination, you could say it was a regicide because he was the heir apparent, although it technically may not have been one.

But the world didn't have to wait long for a true regicide and when it happened, it was arguably the most impactful regicide not just in modern history, but in the history of the world.

Remember how Austria-Hungary declared war on Serbia and then Russia declared war on Austria-Hungary, starting World War I? Russia really had no business being involved in any major war at that point in its history, which brings us to this next tragedy.

Russia was poor, it was suffering from shortages in clothing, weapons, and food, and its infrastructure was a mess, from the railroads to the telegraph lines.

Even in 1914, there wasn't much infrastructure in Russia outside Moscow, St. Petersburg, and a few other cities, which created logistical nightmares for the military moving soldiers to and from the front.

The navy was years behind even the German Navy, which has never been known as a maritime power, and Russia's overall industrial capacity was close to Austria-Hungary's but far behind Germany's.

So, what did the Russians have going for them at the start of World War I?

Well, the Russians had a lot of men, and they had an autocratic ruler, Tsar Nicholas II.

By all accounts, Nicholas was a nice, family guy. All the surviving pictures of him, and a few films, usually show him in the warm embrace of his family: wife Alexandra, son Alexei, and daughters Olga, Tatiana, Maria, and Anastasia. They truly were a happy family, laughing and frolicking on the grounds of the royal palace, but it was the quiet before the storm. They were the last in the line of the Russian Romanov Dynasty that began more than 300 years earlier, in 1613.

You've no doubt heard the term "history repeats itself", right? Well, it's a bit of a simple and clichéd way to view all of world history, but there is some truth to it in some cases, especially with the Romanov family. In many ways, Nicholas was a lot like Marie Antoinette.

As Russia wrestled with poverty and social problems (remember the Russian loss in the Russo-Japanese War and the failed 1905 Revolution in Russia?), Nicholas seemed oblivious. Instead of dealing with the problems in his backyard, he made the fateful decision to enter a war that only made the domestic problems worse.

And his enemies quickly took advantage.

On March 8, 1917, a coalition of angry soldiers, disgruntled factor workers, and political leftists took to the streets of Petrograd (St. Petersburg) to protest the war and the tsar's autocratic hold on the country. The revolution ended on March 16 with the Tsar abdicating the throne in favor of a government ruled by a coalition of political moderates and communist factions such as Mensheviks and the Bolsheviks.

The Romanov family was sent away to live under house arrest and were moved around the vast country.

But the new government kept Russia in the war, which proved to be a fatal mistake for the Romanov family as well as millions of Russians.

It's important to point out here that the socialists, anarchists, and communists that comprised Russia's left-wing in 1917 were not a united front. Many of them hated each other and often refused to cooperate, even in the face of common enemies. But the Bolsheviks, who were led by Vladimir Lenin and Leon Trotsky, were the best organized and were able to put aside their differences with other factions, at least temporarily.

The Bolsheviks organized workers and soldiers on the streets of Moscow and St. Petersburg to shut the cities down, allowing them to seize the government on March 7, 1917.

Lenin was the new head of the government, and his first act was to end Russia's involvement in the war.

His second act was to do something about the Romanov family.

After moving the Romanovs to different locations, the Bolsheviks finally brought them to their final home in July 1918 in the city of Yekaterinburg in the Ural Mountains. The Romanovs were allowed to linger for days until on the night of July 16 they were rounded up, along with four of their retainers, and brought to the basement of the mansion that had been their home.

They were then lined up against a wall and shot repeatedly by a Bolshevik firing squad. When the smoke cleared and some of the Romanov children were still alive, the soldiers were ordered to stab and beat the survivors.

Later, the bodies of the royal family were dismembered and buried in an unmarked grave to keep them from becoming martyrs.

Lenin and the Bolsheviks, who by then were simply known as communists, denied the rumors of the regicide for years until they finally won the Russian Civil War in 1922, consolidating communist power in Russia.

The death of the Romanovs ensured that the communists would take over power in Russia and impose their new form of government first on Russia, and later on most of the other countries in Eastern Europe. Among Lenin's most trusted enforcers was Joseph Stalin, who came to power in 1924 and was the man most responsible for forming the Soviet Union.

The Soviet Union existed for nearly 70 years, costing the lives of millions of people through forced starvation, war, and other forms of repression.

The regicide of the Romanovs *did* have the effect of making them martyrs, no matter what Lenin, Stalin, and the communists attempted.

The Romanovs became saints in the Russian Orthodox Church and are today remembered fondly by the Russian people, who try to balance their often tumultuous and conflicting history in a way that respects all elements of their past.

THE BIG CRASH

October 24 1929 was one of the most destructive days in world history. There wasn't a major battle that day, or a terrorist attack, no major political figure was assassinated, and few if any people directly connected to this event died on that day (although plenty did later). Still, there's no doubt that the world changed tremendously on that day.

That day is commonly known today as "Black Thursday," which is the day when the stock market crashed by more than 11% of its volume. But that was just the beginning; by July 1932, the stock market had lost 89% of its volume, signaling the beginning of the Great Depression.

Although the global economy was far less global in 1929, and even many elements of the US economy were still self-sufficient and somewhat isolated, Black Thursday created a ripple of negative effects throughout the world.

If it had just been the stock market crash, the global economy probably could have survived it much better. Far fewer people were involved in the stock market at that time, and most were affluent, but enough money was tied up in the stock market that it directly affected other sectors of the economy.

The swinging lifestyle that many people enjoyed in the 1920s was often funded on credit (yes, some things never change!), which led to a credit crunch and a bubble that popped when the stock market crashed.

The banks refused to give loans out of fear after the crash, stifling any economic growth that may have mitigated the effects of the crash. Then to make things worse, people began drawing their money out of the banks, which in the era before the FDIC existed to insure banks, caused many banks to close.

And many people suddenly saw their life savings disappear.

Because there was no money or credit, or even many banks by the mid-1930s, the real estate market collapsed. Industrial factories also closed, and in an effort to regain some of their losses, many banks began recalling loans, which further bankrupted millions of individuals and businesses.

Then the Dust Bowl storms hit the lower Great Plains throughout most of the 1930s. Although the Dust Bowl was caused by a combination of severe drought and poor farming techniques in the dry region and wasn't the result of the stock market crash, it became a part of the vicious economic cycle of the era. During any other time, the Dust Bowl would have been much less of a problem, but during the Great Depression, it was tremendously aggravated and in turn, made the Depression much worse in the US.

Millions of Americans then went on the move. So-called 'Oakies' from the Great Plains went to California and Blacks from the Deep South went to the Midwest and Northeast.

The Great Depression may have started in the US, but it quickly reached Europe. By 1932, there were 14 million unemployed in the US, six million in Germany, and three million in the United Kingdom.

Perhaps the greatest impact of the stock market crash was that overnight millions of people began turning to far left and far-right political parties for answers. Suddenly, communists and fascists made a lot more sense to the average person, which began to play out in the streets and polls across the world in the 1930s.

HOW NONVIOLENT PROTEST WAS BORN

A few months after the stock market crashed in the US, a new social and political movement formed in India that would shake the world. On March 12, 1930, a relatively unknown Indian lawyer and community leader named Mahatma Gandhi began leading a group of 78 men from his ashram in the city of Ahmedabad on a march 239 miles south to the city of Dandi on the west coast of India in the state of Gujarat.

This was no ordinary march. Gandhi led this march to protest against the British salt laws, which gave the British complete control of the collection, manufacturing, and sales of salt. And although salt can be found in plentiful locations in coastal areas due to evaporation, Indians were prohibited from collecting it. Salt taxes comprised over 8% of the British tax revenue in India, so any disruption of this industry would hurt the British government's bottom line.

But by the time the Salt March, as it became known, wrapped up on April 6, it had grown in size and stature, threatening Britain's long-term control of India.

India's journey to the Salt March didn't happen overnight. Once again, let's go back a bit to one of our earlier important events. If you'll remember, 1526 was a major year in India's history, as that was when the Muslim Mughals conquered northern India. Mughal rule was strong until the Mughal emperor, Aurangzeb, died in 1707.

Aurangzeb's death initiated internal power struggles among the Mughals as well as inviting European colonial powers to establish port colonies, similar to what they would later do in China.

Much of the early European colonial forces were actually funded and led by government-subsidized private companies, such as the British East India Company. The British East India Company established beach heads along the east coast and in Bengal in the mid-1700s, and by the early 1800s, it had made Britain the sole colonial power in India.

In 1858, after the major anti-British uprising (Sepoy Rebellion) took place across northern India, control of the country was transferred from the British East India Company to the British Crown. Although the Crown generally tried to include local elites in the power structure and undertook infrastructure programs to help the Indian people, it was the era of nationalism and socialism.

Those concepts may have originated in Europe, but they were becoming popular in many European colonies such as India. In 1885, the nationalist organization, the Indian National Congress (INC) was formed, setting the Indian people on a collision course with the British authorities.

It was certainly inevitable that a collision would occur, but how that collision happened would determine the course of history.

In 1930, Gandhi was 61 years of age and had already been a successful lawyer and activist in South Africa and India. He had risen through the ranks of the INC and taken a leadership role when he was given the task of leading a major protest.

Gandhi and his 78 followers left on their march with few expectations, some provisions, and wearing their white khadi gowns. The only true expectation they had was that all the marchers would follow the concept of satyagraha, or "peace force."

Satyagraha came to define the movement's non-violent resistance to British rule.

The marchers were quickly joined by thousands more marchers also wearing khadi, and similar marches began forming all across India. The march then became an international news story and something the British really didn't know how to deal with.

The British were used to cracking skulls in their colonies, so when Gandhi and his followers peacefully marched to the sea, they didn't know how to react. When Gandhi finally reached the sea, he picked up some mud from the ground and said, "With this, I am shaking the foundations of the British Empire." He then broke the law by boiling the mud in water, producing salt.

The immediate ramifications of Gandhi's Salt March weren't exactly earth-shaking. The salt tax continued and so too did British rule until 1947.

But things were changing underneath the surface. The Indian independence movement grew exponentially after the Salt March and gained plenty of support from outside India. The Salt March also ensured that Gandhi would lead INC in the future.

Finally, and perhaps most importantly, the Salt March changed how people protested. The idea of non-violent protest wasn't necessarily unknown before Gandhi, but he made it a tactic employed by later protesters such as Martin Luther King Junior. The term satyagraha may never have achieved mainstream recognition, but the idea of non-violently opposing what you believe are injustices did.

THE HISTORIC
ELECTIONS OF 1932

As the world descended further into the Great Depression, two very important elections took place that year that would decide the course of the world for the following 13 years. The US presidential election of 1860 may have been the most important election in US history, but the elections in 1932, especially in Germany and the United States, proved to be the most crucial in world history.

Once the elections of 1932 were over, the path that the world was on became clearer, although not necessarily better.

Let's begin in Germany. At the time, it was still a unified country but had suffered from many problems after World War I. A devastating cycle of hyperinflation in the early 1920s caused extreme poverty and political turmoil that the post-imperial government - known as the Weimar Republic for the city where the new government assembly first met - was unable to handle.

By the late 1920s, Germans were turning from the mainstream political parties to the far-left German Communist Party and the far-right German National Socialist Workers' Party (Nazis for short) for answers. As those two diametrically-opposed parties grew in numbers, gaining more and more seats in the elected assembly known as the Reichstag, so too did political violence.

But both sides seemed to feed on the violence, and both groups were led by charismatic men: Adolf Hitler for the Nazis and Ernst Thälmann for the Communists.

And if you remember, Germany also experienced the Great Depression, but they experienced the equivalent of the US Roaring '20s.

The Golden Twenties, also known as the Happy Twenties, is a short five-year time period within the decade of the 1920s in Germany. The era began in 1924 after the end of the hyperinflation following World War I and ended with the Wall Street Crash of 1929.

But all of Germany's political, economic, and social problems came to a head on July 31, 1932, during the federal elections.

The final tally had the Nazis as the party with the most seats at 230 and the highest percentage of the vote with 37%. The Communists came in third with 89 seats and 14%. Hitler had just lost the presidential election to the political fossil Paul von Hindenburg in April but winning the most votes in the Reichstag was a nice consolation prize. With that said, it wasn't a majority, so Hitler and the Nazis were unable to form a new government.

So, another election was held on November 6, 1932.

The Nazis lost 34 seats and the Communists gained 11 seats, but the Nazis remained the number one party. After some negotiations with center-right parties, Hitler was finally able to achieve his goal of taking control of the government. Hindenburg remained a figurehead until 1934 when Hitler became the Fuhrer.

Just two days after Germany's historic election, on November 8, the United States had its presidential and congressional elections. Although the political, social, and economic situation in the US was much less violent in 1932 than it was in Germany, it was still very desperate. Incumbent Republican President Herbert Hoover appeared weak and helpless in the midst of the Great Depression and the Republican-controlled Congress was also seen as out of touch with the American people.

So, the American people elected Democrat challenger Franklin Roosevelt in a landslide and flipped the House of Representatives and Senate from Republican to Democrat control.

Once Roosevelt was in office and he had congressional support, he was able to initiate his "New Deal," which used the power of the government to put people to work. Programs such as the Tennessee Valley Authority brought power to many people in the South, and also gave thousands of jobs, while the Works Progress Administration put unemployed Americans to work doing everything from building the Hoover Dam to art.

Over in Germany, the Nazis also initiated several, similar programs, such as building the freeway system known as the Autobahn and subsidizing companies like Volkswagen.

But there's where the similarities ended.

The elections of 1932 in Germany and the United States ensured that both countries would pursue national visions that may have had some similarities but were, in the end, very different. As the 1930s progressed and both countries slowly worked themselves out of the Great Depression – literally - their political and ideological differences became a gulf.

Eventually, that gulf would be too large to bridge, becoming one of the major factors that led to World War II.

MAO'S LONG MARCH

When the Chinese Civil War broke out in 1927, most people around the world didn't give it much thought. Outside of the port cities, Westerners didn't know much about China and didn't really care. It was a mysterious land that was very exotic and alien to most and best left alone. Napoleon himself recognized this, plus China's potentially powerful characteristics, referring to it as a sleeping giant that should be left alone.

And for several hundred years, the Chinese preferred to be left alone. However, when the treaty ports started to open up China to foreign trade, new ideas began to enter the land of the sleeping dragon.

Ideas like Marxism, socialism, and communism.

Karl Marx's ideas were originally intended for a more urban audience, and he believed factory workers would lead the future communist revolutions, which is what happened in Russia. In other countries with sizable communist parties, most members were also urban factory workers, so China, which was overwhelming agrarian in the 1920s, was not believed by most experts to be a potential target of communism.

But once again, the experts were wrong.

A new type of peasant-centric communism formed in China that was influenced by the leadership and writings of Mao Zedong, who would later become the first leader of the People's Republic of China (communist China). But Mao would have to survive the Chinese Civil War first, which brings us to our next major event in modern history.

The Chinese Civil War pitted the communists on one side against the nationalists, who were led by Chiang Kai-Shek, on the other. The war began when the central government deteriorated, and extremists turned to bullets over the ballot box.

I'm sure by now you see that was a theme throughout the world in the 1920s.

Although most of the world knew little about the war taking place in China, the Soviet Union was ahead of the curve, sending advisors. Germany, first the Weimar government and then the Nazis, likewise supported the nationalist army.

Foreign support played a key role early in the Civil War and almost led to the defeat of the Red Army (the communist army). A German military advisor to Chiang Kai-shek, Nationalist Army, Hans von Seeckt devised a plan whereby the nationalist forces would use their superior numbers to encircle and destroy the Red Army in what became known as the "Encirclement Campaigns."

The Jiangxi and Fujian provinces in southern China became a hotly contested region, as it was a communist stronghold that if defeated could give the nationalists victory. After four unsuccessful encirclements, the nationalists besieged the region for a fifth time, from September 25, 1933, to October 10, 1934.

The fifth time was the charm!

The nationalists took back the region, but the Red Army slipped past them and began what became known as the Long March. About 80,000 Red Army soldiers, led by Mao and others, made a more than 5,600-mile trek west and then north across rivers, over mountains, and around lakes to reach their base in the mountainous Shensi province in northern China.

The Long March began on October 16, 1934, and finally ended on October 22, 1935.

The effects of the Long March weren't immediately apparent, but within a few years, they became quite obvious.

Maybe the most important result of the Long March is that it helped catapult Mao to the leadership of the Chinese Communist Party, which meant he became leader of China when the communist forces finally won the war. Mao then went on to become the face of the developing world's version of communism by supporting various communist insurgencies in Asia, Africa, and Latin America.

Mao's special brand of communism, which favored rural peasants over urban workers, even earned its own name - Maoism.

But as much as Mao was seen as a defender of oppressed masses of the Third World, he also moved China away from the Soviet Union and closer to the United States.

Logistically speaking, the Long March allowed the Red Army to regroup and replenish its numbers. The communists and nationalists actually formed an alliance from 1936 to 1945 to fight the Japanese, who had invaded parts of China, which gave the Red Army more opportunities to hone their military skills, especially in guerilla activities.

And this brings up several "what if" scenarios.

If the nationalists had totally destroyed the Red Army in the Fifth Encirclement, would the nationalists have been able to resist the Japanese alone?

If the nationalists were able to defeat the communists and the Japanese, what would China look like today?

If a leader other than Mao had come to the forefront of the communists, would he have been as influential throughout the world?

These are all interesting questions to ponder, proving that the Long March was definitely one of the most important events in modern history.

"A DAY THAT WILL
LIVE IN INFAMY"

Our history of the most important events in modern history brings us now to World War II. There are a lot of events that took place during World War II that are more than deserving of being on our list. Germany's initial attack on Poland on September 1, 1939, was definitely pretty big.

Then there was France's fall on June 25, 1940, and the Dunkirk evacuation right before it.

Germany's invasion of the Soviet Union, on June 22, 1941, was also a major event with monumental impacts.

There are also several other events from the war you could add to this list, but for the sake of brevity, I'm going to narrow things down to two events. The first was the Japanese attack on Pearl Harbor, Hawaii on December 7, 1941.

Many Americans think that the Pearl Harbor attack was a "sneak attack" or that it came without warning. Although most Americans didn't expect it on that lazy Sunday morning, tensions had been building between the United States and Japan, as well as the US and Germany, since the 1930s.

On September 19, 1931, Japan invaded Manchuria, which was the true start of World War II, at least in the Pacific. The Japanese then invaded Nanking (aka Nanjing), China in 1937 as well as other parts of the country.

If you'll remember, the Chinese nationalists and communists called a truce at this point to fight the Japanese, but there was little they could do against the mighty Japanese military without outside help. They managed to get some support from the Soviet Union, but most of what they received in firepower came from the United States after 1940.

Although the US was still officially neutral in World War II, it was providing arms to China, the Soviet Union, and the United Kingdom in the lend-lease program. The Axis Powers, especially Japan, weren't very happy.

But relations between Japan and the US had been deteriorating for some time. When the Japanese invaded Nanking and massacred a large number of the civilian population, they also bombed the US gunboat *Panay*. A Japanese soldier then assaulted US ambassador John Wilson in Nanking in 1938, further adding to the tensions.

Political and ideological differences also played a role in the tensions. Japan's government followed an ideology that mixed militarism with emperor worship and ancient Shintoism to create an Asian version of fascism. They were also aligned with Germany, Italy, and the European Axis Powers.

So, when President Roosevelt ordered the Pacific Fleet moved from San Diego to Hawaii, the Japanese thought the Americans were planning to attack first. That didn't happen, but when France fell to Germany, the US ended all oil exports to Japan, and that made conflict between the two nations almost certainly inevitable.

For Americans, Canadians, Saudis, Russians, or many other nations who produce plenty of oil, having an imported source may hurt, but it wouldn't be the end of the world. But for Japan, which was and still is heavily dependent upon imports, it was an act of war.

So, when the Japanese attacked Pearl Harbor, it really shouldn't have come as quite as much of a surprise. But there's no doubt it *was* a shock to most Americans, and it shook the very fabric of a country that hadn't experienced a major foreign invasion since the War of 1812.

When the smoke of the two waves of Japanese attacks cleared, the devastation was massive. Four of the US's battleships were sunk, 188 aircraft were destroyed, numerous other ships and planes were damaged, and 2,335 Americans were killed, including 63 civilians.

President Roosevelt addressed the nation the next day on the radio, stating that December 7, "would be a date that lived in infamy." The US then promptly declared war on Japan. Germany and Italy then declared war on the US on December 11, putting the US officially into both theaters of World War II.

There's no doubt that the Japanese attack on Pearl Harbor was massive, but did it have the intended effect?

The simple answer is a resounding no!

Yes, the Japanese took out some American battleships and damaged quite a few other ships, but the damaged ships were quickly rebuilt, and battleships weren't as integral to the war in the Pacific as they were in Europe and North Africa. Aircraft carriers and marine landings on small Pacific islands were the primary strategies the US employed in the Pacific, and their capabilities were not damaged in that respect. American aircraft carriers were the primary target of the Japanese, and they all avoided the attack, as they were out to sea and couldn't be located.

The Pearl Harbor attack also galvanized the American public, changing their attitude from strongly neutral to pro-war overnight. The war effort went into overdrive, and America's immense resources and manpower was quickly put to use in Europe and the Pacific to help the Allies win the war.

Then there was the case of Germany and Italy.

Since they had an alliance with Japan, they apparently felt obligated to declare war on the US. Of course, that didn't work out well for them, but it's difficult to say if things would have been different if they hadn't declared war. Maybe the US would have just gone ahead and declared war on them first anyway.

Or maybe the US would have focused all its attention on the Pacific.

Whatever the case, there's no doubt that the Japanese attack on Pearl Harbor was probably *the* biggest event in World War II because after that, things went rapidly downhill for the Axis Powers.

HIROSHIMA AND NAGASAKI USHER IN THE ATOMIC AGE

On May 8, 1945, Germany officially surrendered to the Allies, ending World War II in Europe. Celebrations immediately erupted in Britain, the US, France, and other places around the world as millions of war-weary people celebrated what became known as Victory in Europe or VE Day.

That's definitely a major date and a very important event, but how the war ended in the Pacific proved to be a bit bigger, and louder.

The Germans put up a bitter fight until the end, but the war in Europe was logistically beneficial to the Allied ground forces, as they were able to surround Berlin with sheer numbers and batter it into submission. The geography of Japan was not conducive to an overwhelming land invasion.

Remember earlier in this book when I explained that Japan's composition as an archipelago made it safe from invasion for most of history? Well, that continued into World War II. The Americans had taken enough islands close to Japan, including the Japanese island of Okinawa, to bomb all of Japan, but landing marines on the main island in a D-Day type of invasion would be extremely costly.

The Allied plan for the amphibious invasion of Japan was known as Operation Downfall, but it had two major drawbacks: the casualty count for the Allies was expected to be in the tens of thousands and the invasion couldn't happen until 1946.

So, American President Harry Truman decided to go with Plan B.

Plan B was the unleashing of atomic/nuclear weapons on Japan. An atomic bomb was successfully detonated for the first time in the world on July 16, 1945, and less than a month later, the US Army dropped two more on major Japanese cities

On August 6, 1945, the American bomber *Enola Gay* dropped the atomic bomb known as Little Boy on the industrial city of Hiroshima, instantly destroying most of the city center and killing up to 66,000 of the city's inhabitants and injuring 69,000 others.

Three days later, on August 9, the US bomber *Bockscar* dropped Little Man on the port city of Nagasaki, killing 39,000 people instantly and injuring 25,000 others.

The two bombings combined was by far the largest death count of any single event in human history. In addition to the immediate death toll, many thousands more died over the next several years from cancer and radiation sickness, while many were born with birth defects.

The bombings did have their intended immediate effect, though. Japan unconditionally surrendered on August 14, after which many of its government and military leaders were tried for war crimes in Tokyo in a similar trial to that of the Nazis in Nuremberg, Germany. The surrender then began a period of heavy US military involvement in Japan, especially in Okinawa, which continues to this day and is not always welcomed by the locals.

The bombings and surrender brought great shame and "loss of face" to Japan, which is about the worst thing that can happen in Japanese culture. With that said, as we looked at earlier in this book, the Japanese are resilient people who adapt continuously to shifting geopolitical situations.

The new Japanese constitution that was written and ratified in 1947 came with an interesting section. Article 9 of the Japanese Constitution outlaws war as a means of settling international disputes. Partly due to that article and also due to conditions imposed on it after the war, Japan has only had a very small military since.

So, they were forced to focus their energies on other things.

After spending almost a decade physically rebuilding their country, Japan emerged as one of the world's leading economic powers by the 1970s.

Finally, the bombings of Hiroshima and Nagasaki ushered in what was called the Atomic Age. Scientists learned how to harness atomic power for good, by using it as a clean and usually safe source of power, while others improved the military capabilities of atomic energy to create weapons that could destroy us all.

A NATION WAS BORN AND AN ETERNAL WAR BEGAN

Another major event that took place during World War II that I didn't cover was the Nazis' attempted genocide of the Jews. Of course, this was more of an ongoing event that began as soon as the Nazis took power and continued until the end of the war, and it certainly had its own impacts, which immediately began being realized after the war.

The Nuremberg Trials were a major result of the attempted genocide of the Jews. But even more important was the creation of the state of Israel. When the state of Israel was declared on May 14, 1948, it was greeted with cheers from millions of Jews worldwide and approval from many times more non-Jewish people who thought it was only right that they should have their own country.

But millions of people weren't exactly happy about the move.

The creation of no other state/country has been as polarizing or as impactful as Israel's. So, let's take a look at how this happened as well as how and why it's impacted the modern world.

Israel's history, of course, began in ancient times, the Bronze Age to be exact. Before 1,200 BCE, what is today Israel was a collection of city-states inhabited by people known as Canaanites. The Egyptians and Hittites were the major powers in the region, though, often ruling the Canaanites until around 1,000 BCE when the ancient Kingdom of Israel formed.

This was the kingdom of David and Solomon.

Eventually, the kingdom fell to the Assyrians, Babylonians, Macedonian Greeks, and Romans in succession. Many of the Israelites mixed with these other populations while some were dispersed and ended up in Europe and other places.

The Jewish communities in Europe and the Middle East often found themselves in conflict with the locals, so in the late 1800s, influenced by European nationalist ideas, a Hungarian Jew named Theodor Herzl came up with his idea of Jewish nationalism that he called Zionism.

Basically, Zionism called for Jews to return to their ancient homeland, which was called Palestine at the time. The problem was, Palestine was ruled by the Ottoman Empire, and they weren't too keen on allowing Jewish migrants into their colony.

But they came anyway. And they kept coming, forming new communities such as Tel Aviv.

The Ottoman Empire was on the losing side of World War I, though, so they lost all of their imperial possessions. Those colonies were divvied up by the League of Nations (the rise and fall of that organization could probably be a chapter in this book) and given to the winners of World War I as "mandates."

Britain was given Palestine, which it soon learned was a headache that it would have rather done without.

Before the British gained possession of Palestine, they were very much in favor of a Jewish homeland in Palestine. The British government even went so far as to issue the "Balfour Declaration" in 1917, named for the British foreign secretary at the time, Arthur Balfour, which declared British support a Jewish homeland.

Here's where things start to get a bit tricky.

There were plenty of non-Jewish Arabs already living in Palestine, and they had been there for centuries. So, the declaration had the effect of angering the Arabs/Palestinians, while also encouraging Jewish immigration to Palestine. Arabs rioted against the British, so in response, the British placed limits on the numbers of Jews allowed to immigrate.

This didn't sit well with the more militant Zionist Jews.

The Zionists formed militant/terrorist groups (Palestine/Israel was probably where the idea of "one man's terrorist is another man's freedom fighter" began), such as the Haganah and Irgun, that targeted Arabs *and* British. The British Minister of State in the Middle East, Walter Guinness, was assassinated by Jewish terrorists, and the King David Hotel in Jerusalem was bombed by the Irgun, killing 91 people.

Okay, so that brief history of Israel brings us to the period just after World War II. Jewish survivors from across Europe began making their way to Palestine and for the most part, the world was sympathetic to their cause. The newly-formed United Nations was also sympathetic to the Jews but didn't want to leave the Arabs out, so it passed a resolution in 1947 that divided Palestine into two separate states.

But the Jews of Palestine didn't wait. The Irgun and Haganah gave the Jews a ready-built army, so on May 14, 1948, Jewish leader David Ben-Gurion unilaterally declared the Jewish state of Israel in what was formerly the British mandate of Palestine.

The announcement sent a wave of reaction throughout the world.

The news was greeted positively in the West and somewhat neutrally in the communist bloc, but in the Arab and Islamic worlds, it meant war. The Arab League, led by Egypt and Syria, attacked Israel, initiating a bloody and brutal war that lasted for nine months.

When it was over, Israel had successfully defended itself.

With the support of the US, Israel was able to build a state-of-the-art military that has defended itself in numerous wars, especially in 1956, 1967, and 1972. The Israeli military has gained a reputation as a true David among many Goliaths.

Israel's precarious existence in the midst of many hostile countries also led to it becoming a nuclear power, although it has never formally admitted to having nukes.

What about the people who were in Israel before the Jews arrived? This question raises perhaps the most enduring impact of the creation of Israel. The status of millions of "Palestinians," who are native Arabs in the region, Muslims and Christians, remains a decisive issue. The plight of the Palestinians has become a political issue across the world and the political spectrum, although it doesn't appear it will be solved anytime soon.

There's little doubt that future wars, terrorism, and/or riots will happen that can be traced to the day Israel officially became a country.

TWO LINES THAT SHOULDN'T HAVE BEEN CROSSED

It should be clear by now that World War II was itself probably *the* biggest game-changer of the modern world. In addition to ushering in the Atomic Age and the state of Israel, many other borders and alliances were reformed after the war.

The West quickly found out that although Joseph Stalin and the Soviet Union may have been really helpful against Germany and Japan, the mustachioed communist dictator wasn't that cool after all.

Stalin immediately became aggressive in Eastern Europe by moving his troops into several countries and ensuring that communist governments were installed. By 1948, it was clear to the world that the Cold War had begun, when Stalin blockaded Berlin for the first time.

Stalin also did the same thing in Asia, invading Korea at the end of the war in 1945 and installing a communist government in the northern part of the peninsula. The situation left Korea divided at the 38th Parallel between communist North Korea and democratic-capitalist South Korea.

And in 1950, China was the wildcard in this situation.

American President Harry Truman was a proponent of meeting communist advances with force if necessary, so he was very clear to the Soviets and Chinese that the 38th Parallel was a line that shouldn't be crossed. And for a few years, it seemed like the communists would be fine with that, but on June 25, 1950, North Korean forces crossed that line and invaded South Korea.

The North Koreans were definitely urged to make this move by the Soviets and the Chinese, who had sent arms and advisors to North Korea. The truth is, though, they should have never crossed that line.

The North Koreans initially surged far into the South, but after the United Nations condemned North Korea and recommended member states get involved, the United States, Britain, and some other countries sent troops to fight North Korea.

The fight was going well for the UN forces when another line was crossed that shouldn't have been.

The commander of the UN forces was General George MacArthur, who was as gung-ho to fight as he was a colorful character. MacArthur was also an ardent anti-communist, so when the American forces began driving north after halting the initial North Korean advance, they had reached the 38th Parallel by October 19. They could've stopped there, but they decided to cross the line.

So, technically it was only one line that was crossed, but it was crossed by *both* sides.

As the Americans led the UN forces north, MacArthur planned to cross the Yalu River into China. But this was a line that even the wily World War II vet couldn't cross. The Chinese Red Army became involved in the war when they got close and pushed the

Americans back to the 38th Parallel where hostilities ended on July 27, 1953.

After all that death and destruction - nearly 200,000 died on the UN side and close to a million on the communist side - the borders remained as they had been when hostilities broke out. Even so, it was a war that produce profound changes in the world.

Despite still being relatively poor and backward, China went on to establish itself as a major player on the geopolitical scene. It would continue to support communist insurgencies and dictatorships throughout the world.

The Korean War also established the United States as *the* new power in the West. In fact, after the Korean War, it became obvious that the new global power structure was a bipolar one, where you were either on the side of the USA or USSR.

The question on most people's minds during the remainder of the 1950s and into the 1960s was "When and where is the next 'Korea' going to happen, and will it turn the Cold War hot?"

A KID FROM MEMPHIS WAS
INTRODUCED TO THE WORLD

Most of the important events we've covered so far in this book have taken place in the arena of politics, military, religion, science, economics, or a combination of these, so let's change pace and look at one of the most important events from popular culture.

The term "popular culture," or "pop culture," is often broadly defined as anything that has to do with the popular tastes of the majority of the population, and can include music, movies, television, comedy, and sometimes consumerism in general. Basically, anything that isn't "high-brow" on the one hand or "folk" on the other is often part of pop culture.

So rock, rap, and country are forms of popular music, while classical music isn't.

The idea of pop culture is a very modern phenomenon and really only caught on after World War II. Radio, TV, and film were the technologies that drove early pop culture and by the 1950s, the new form of music known as rock n' roll emerged in the US to become the premier form.

Rock, as it became known, mixed many elements of older folk music, from negro spirituals to bluegrass, as well as some early forms of pop music including country and Mississippi blues and rhythm and blues to become rock, or as early rockstars called it, "rockabilly." By the mid-1950s, rock/rockabilly had emerged from Black juke joints in the South and a few shady pool halls here and there in the North, to get some major air play on radio stations and become a legitimate style of pop music.

Well, not quite legitimate.

There were still taboos associated with rock music at that time, as it clearly had allusions toward sex (rock n' roll is, after all, a euphemism for — well, you don't have to think long on that one!) and a general rebellious nature. Others didn't like the music style's association with Black America, especially at a time when the civil rights movement was starting.

So, no one would've guessed that on September 9, 1956, a poor 21-year-old White kid from the Memphis projects would change the pop culture world with one TV performance. But that's exactly what happened when Elvis Presley took the stage that night. Few people in the US knew his name before that performance, but afterwards, he became known around the world.

Elvis Aaron Presley's journey began when he was born in Tupelo, Mississippi on January 8, 1935, to Vernon and Gladys Presley. It was the Great Depression and Vernon struggled to make ends meet, so he moved his family to nearby Memphis, Tennessee for better opportunities. Although Vernon found work in Memphis, the cost of living was higher in the city, so the Presley family was forced to live in public housing.

But for young Elvis, Memphis was a land of incredible opportunities.

Elvis spent his time learning to play the guitar and hanging out on Beale Street, where he learned the blues from that neighborhood's many black street performers. He also sang at his church, learning traditional gospel music, and being a White Southerner in the late 1940s and early 1950s, he had plenty of exposure to country music as well.

Elvis eventually molded all these musical styles to make his own sound, lay down a record at Sun Studios in Memphis, and begin making a name for himself in the music scene.

But that's only the beginning of the story. Elvis' manager, the shady yet colorful Colonel Parker, got the crooner several TV performances in 1956. He appeared on the popular *Milton Berle Show* and *The Steve Allen Show* earlier that year before going on to make the big appearance on CBS's *Ed Sullivan Show*.

Although Charles Laughton was filling in for Sullivan that night, who was recovering from a car accident, it didn't matter. America tuned in to see "Elvis the Pelvis" as he was being called, not Sullivan or Laughton. A record 82.6% of the TV audience, or 60 million people watched Elvis perform his "light rock," heavily gospel-inspired song, "Love Me Tender" that night.

Elvis' performance made him a household name and catapulted him to international fame. The act also helped rock become a mainstream style of pop music. Elvis would go on to set many precedents that we see with rockstars today.

Elvis was the first rockstar to have a comeback. Actually, he had two: the first when he returned from military service in 1960 and another in 1968 after a new generation no longer saw him as "cool."

There's no doubt that Elvis was also the first global rockstar. Although Canada was the only foreign country the "King" played in, he was, and remains, popular on every continent.

Elvis was also the first rockstar to *attempt* an acting career. The movies he starred in may not have been great - most weren't even good! - and his acting skills were average at best, but hey, he was the first to give it a go!

Elvis also helped make the television the dominant medium in the world. Ten years after his performance, the vast majority of Americans had TVs in their homes. Elvis also did some of the first true music videos.

Not bad for a poor kid from the tough streets of Memphis.

HOW THE IRON CURTAIN BECAME OFFICIAL

Elvis was drafted into the US Army in 1958, in the early stages of the Cold War, and sent to West Germany on what would have been the front lines of any major action in Europe. As Americans were glued to their TV sets to see Elvis' new "buzz cut," the leaders of the Soviet Union and their communist allies in Eastern Europe, known as the Warsaw Pact, were planning to consolidate their power.

The leaders of East Germany in particular quickly learned that many of their people were willing to risk quite a bit, even their lives, to get over to the West. So, for many people, the city of West Berlin was a kind of oasis of freedom in the middle of the totalitarian communist countries.

But for the Soviets and the other communist countries, West Berlin was a thorn in their side.

It was an island of capitalism and democracy behind the "Iron Curtain" of communism they had erected just after World War II, and they wanted nothing more than to add West Berlin to the growing number of lands that were becoming communist at the time.

The Soviets and East Germans first attempted to blockade West Berlin in 1948, which the West defeated with round-the-clock supply flights. Stalin eventually relented but his successor, Nikita Khrushchev, gave an ultimatum to the Western powers to leave West Berlin in 1958 or face a Soviet invasion.

US President Eisenhower called Khrushchev's bluff, backing the dictator down.

But Khrushchev reissued the threat on June 4, 1961, to the new US president, John F. Kennedy. Khrushchev thought that since Kennedy was young, he could push him around, but Kennedy also called his bluff.

But Khrushchev had to do something to save face, so he got together with the leaders of East Germany and on August 13, 1961, the Berlin Wall began being built.

The tensions quickly turned into a crisis, with Soviet and American tanks squaring off at the border station known as "Checkpoint Charlie." The tanks were only yards from each other and at any moment shooting could have started World War III.

Thankfully, though, cooler heads prevailed, and the tanks were pulled back. Citizens of West Berlin were allowed to travel through East Germany to get to West Germany (West Berlin was basically an island in the middle of East Germany), but free travel was still verboten to East Germans.

But when freedom is only yards away, people will take great risks for a taste.

East Germans dug tunnels, rushed Checkpoint Charlie, and scaled the Wall to get to West Berlin, with many dying in the process. The Checkpoint Charlie Museum gives the number at 245 deaths, though this includes suicides by border guards and bodies found in the water even when there was no obvious link to them being an escapee. They also state that the first person to die at the Wall was, in fact, an East German officer who committed suicide. But non-official estimates put the death count closer to 500.

The Berlin Wall Crisis was the last Cold War conflict in Europe over Berlin, but it wouldn't be the final, or the scariest, between Kennedy and Khrushchev. The geographic focus of the Cold War would move closer to the US and become much more intense.

ON THE EDGE OF ANNIHILATION

There's no doubt that Khrushchev thought he could bully the younger Kennedy on the world stage. Perhaps he planned to metaphorically slap the American president around a bit before getting what he wanted and then return to Moscow to sip on some vodka and eat a little caviar and borscht.

But just as Khrushchev's energetic exterior often betrayed a man who was quite thoughtful and cunning, Kennedy's youthful looks covered for a man who was quite experienced in the ways of the world.

Kennedy was a World War II veteran who saw action in the Pacific and as a member of the powerful Kennedy family, he was quite familiar with political battles as well.

So, as soon as Kennedy took the oath of office of the presidency in 1961, he and Khrushchev were bound to clash.

The first clash took place in 1961 when Kennedy gave the green light for an attempted invasion of Cuba by anti-Castro, anti-communist dissidents trained and funded by the CIA. The invasion called the Bay of Pigs took place between April 17-20, but it was brutally put down by the communist forces.

Fidel Castro and Khrushchev 1, Kennedy 0.

We just looked at round two in the ongoing battle of wills between Khrushchev and Kennedy: The Berlin Wall Crisis. Let's call that one a draw.

The final showdown between these two men returned to Cuba and was for all the marbles, more or less. The showdown actually began in Turkey, which was a US ally and member of NATO in early 1962. Khrushchev learned that US nuclear missiles that could reach Moscow had been placed in Turkey.

This was too much for Khrushchev, who decided to bring the Cold War to America's backyard by ordering medium-range nuclear missiles to be placed in Cuba. American U-2 spy planes quickly discovered the silos being built in the country, which is only 90 miles from Key West, Florida. That was just too close for Kennedy, so the tensest 12 days in the history of the modern world began.

From October 16 to October 28, 1962, the world waited breathlessly to see if World War III would happen, and during that time, it had moved closer to war than at any other point in the Cold War. Kennedy ordered a naval blockade of Cuba and NATO, and Warsaw Pact troops went on high alert in Europe.

After some negotiating, plenty of threats, and a couple of close calls, the two sides came to an agreement on October 28. To avoid the prospect of nuclear annihilation, Kennedy agreed to remove US nukes from Turkey and in return, Khrushchev would call off his Cuba project, whether or not Castro liked it. When all offensive missiles and the Ilyushin Il-28 light bombers had been withdrawn from Cuba, the blockade was formally ended on November 20, 1962.

The Cuban Missile Crisis opened the world's eyes to the destructiveness of nuclear weapons and just how close everything was to the brink of destruction.

On a positive note, the Cuban Missile Crisis also demonstrated how diplomacy beats bombs, especially in the Cold War era when a few bombs could equal the end of it all. The famed "hotline" phone was installed in Washington and Moscow to allow the leaders of the US and USSR to communicate directly with each other and for a while, relations between the United States and the Soviet Union improved.

THE END OF CAMELOT

After the threat of the Cuban Missile Crisis was avoided, President Kennedy focused more on his domestic agenda, which he coined the "New Frontier." It was a bold new vision that combined politically progressive policies, such as increased social spending, support for civil rights legislation, and urban renewal programs with more traditionally conservative ideas that included tax cuts, tough anti-crime measures, and increased military spending.

Kennedy was the perfect person to promote the bold, new agenda. He was relatively young, had an attractive wife and two cute kids, and was the first true "TV president." Kennedy catapulted to the presidency by rhetorically slapping around his Republican opponent, sitting Vice President Richard Nixon, on the nation's first-ever televised presidential debate.

Kennedy had an amazing story as a young man from a privileged family who did his duty alongside Americans of all backgrounds during World War II. He commanded small patrol torpedo (PT) boats in the Pacific. Kennedy saw combat and heroically rescued several of his crew on one occasion and numerous marines on other occasions.

So, by early 1963, as America seemed to be on the right track under Kennedy, his presidency was nicknamed as "Camelot" by many who compared it to the semi-mythical British King Arthur's court.

But unfortunately, the American Camelot ended on November 22, 1963, in Dallas, Texas.

On that afternoon, President Kennedy was killed by an assassin's bullet, presumably shot by Lee Harvey Oswald, making him the fourth American president to have been assassinated. The fallout from the assassination was immediate and continued for many years.

The first repercussion was that Vice President Lyndon Johnson became the president. Although Johnson continued most of Kennedy's domestic policies, he even more vigorously promoted civil rights legislation.

Johnson also began sending more troops to an otherwise little-known country in southeast Asia called Vietnam. The Vietnam War would cost more than 50,000 Americans their lives, but even worse it divided the nation and left social and political scars that still exist.

President Kennedy's assassination also ended the era of innocence in America. The early 1960s were still quite a bit like the '50s, but after Kennedy's assassination, all of the hallmarks of the 1960s, from the counterculture to the civil rights movement to changes in music, clothes, and hairstyles all rapidly took hold.

Finally, people began questioning the government and the mainstream media more after the Kennedy assassination. Although most people didn't believe there was a conspiracy by well-connected people to kill the president, many had a feeling that they weren't being told the complete story. These questions led to the Warren Commission being formed to conduct investigations and write a report in 1964 that named Oswald as 'a lone gunman'.

The Warren Commission, of course, gave birth to numerous conspiracy theories that centered around the "lone gunman theory" and how plausible, or not, it was. Some of those theories were outlined in Oliver Stone's epic 1991 film, *JFK*.

The Cold War continued after Kennedy's assassination, but proxy wars in places such as Vietnam and Afghanistan (we'll get to that later) took the place of direct standoffs in places such as Berlin and Cuba.

And the Cold War also went into outer space in the 1960s.

"ONE SMALL STEP FOR MANKIND"

Another consequence of the Cold War was the "Space Race" between the USA and USSR. The Space Race actually came about largely due to the Nazis, who developed the first rocket that traveled into space as well as some of the earliest jet airplanes. When the war ended, the Americans snatched up as many German rocket scientists as they could, such as Wernher von Braun, to start NASA.

The Soviets also acquired German rocket scientists, often at gunpoint, to augment their already existing rocket program.

The scene was set for the two new world powers to explore and exploit space for the benefit of their countries and the ideologies they promoted. The winner of the Space Race would achieve worldwide prestige and the bragging rights that theirs was the superior ideology.

Winning the Space Race could also give the winner a strategic advantage. Spy satellites were possible outcomes for those who controlled space.

The first victory went to the Soviets when they successfully launched the first artificial satellite to orbit the Earth, Sputnik, on

October 4, 1957. Needless to say, this was a major development that led to the creation of NASA in the US. Americans were afraid that it was only a matter of time until missiles were put up there.

Well, that type of technology was still a long way off, but the average person didn't know that, so Sputnik's launch contributed to the Red Scare that was sweeping across America in the 1950s. And things didn't get any better when just a month later, on November 3, the Soviets launched the first animal into space, a gentle, unsuspecting pooch named Laika.

The final straw for the Americans came when Soviet cosmonaut (that's what they called their astronauts), Yuri Gagarin, became the first human in space and lived to talk about it, on April 12, 1961. The level of panic in the US increased tremendously. Although most scientists knew the Soviets were still a very long way from putting nukes up in space, American politicians felt they had to show some initiative, so President Kennedy worked with Congress to create the Apollo Program in 1961.

Named after the Greek god of the Sun, the sole goal of the Apollo Program was to put men on the moon.

NASA knew this would be no easy, nor cheap task.

The total cost of the program was $25.4 billion by 1973, which is more than $150 billion in today's dollars. And the program was almost cancelled just as it started when a tragic accident killed all three members of the Apollo 1 crew on January 27, 1967, before it even launched.

But the 1960s was an era of optimism, and when combined with early Soviet space success and the fact that it was the middle of the Cold War, NASA continued with the program.

Then finally, on July 20, 1969, the crew members of the Apollo 11 mission - Neil Armstrong and Buzz Aldrin - walked on the surface of the Moon as their module pilot Michael Collins orbited the satellite. Armstrong and Aldrin planted the American flag, played some golf, and then Armstrong uttered the iconic quote, "That's one small step for man, one giant leap for mankind."

The three men returned to Earth heroes, not immediately aware of just how impactful their mission was on modern history.

The first impact was seen on live TV. Millions of people around the world watched as Armstrong and Aldrin did their work in front of cameras that were placed on the landing module, the *Eagle*, which then beamed the images back to Earth.

It was a demonstration of how far television technology had progressed from being something rarely found in people's homes to broadcasts live from the Moon in less than 20 years!

All of this made everyone stop and consider the magnitude of Apollo 11's mission from the perspective of the danger inherent with it as well as the numerous unknown "X" factors.

Earlier in this book, I compared Magellan's voyage to the Apollo 11 mission, which cannot be stressed enough. Just as Magellan went into the unknown for the first time, blazing new paths for others to follow, so too did the Apollo 11 astronauts.

And like Magellan, there was nothing to save the Apollo astronauts out there if something went wrong.

Perhaps somewhat surprisingly, the first Moon landing didn't set off a rush of lunar exploration. The last manned lunar landing was Apollo 17 in 1972; after that, all lunar missions have been unmanned.

One unintended effect of the Apollo 11 mission was that it brought people closer.

Although the Apollo 11 mission was a success, things could've gone a few different ways. The Americans could have rubbed the Soviets' noses in it, or the Soviets could have freaked out and kicked the Cold War into overdrive. Instead, both sides decided to work together in space for the common good of the planet.

The joint American-Soviet space mission known as Apollo-Soyuz launched on July 15, 1975, bringing together three astronauts from an Apollo crew and two cosmonauts from a Soyuz crew in outer space. The men exchanged handshakes and other pleasantries for the camera, before going on their separate ways about two days later.

The Apollo-Soyuz mission marked the beginning of a détente or thawing in the Cold War during the 1970s, which began with the Apollo 11 touched down on the surface of the Moon.

HOW SOME NERDS IN A GARAGE CHANGED THE WORLD

Earlier in this book, we looked at the invention of the telephone and pondered the question of where we'd be without it. There's no doubt that Alexander Graham Bell got things rolling with his early telephone patent and later perfection of the device, but let's face it, our phones today are more computer than they are phones.

We check our emails on our phones.

We send and receive text messages on our phones.

We surf the web on our phones.

We bank, order food, shop, check sports scores and look at the weather on our phones.

In fact, for many of us, our phones function as traditional phones very little. Truly, the modern smartphone is as much a product of the Computer Age as it is a descendent of Graham's original invention. The day when computers became widely available through what was at the time the upstart company Apple Computers was truly a leap forward in human history…or not!

The idea of a "computer" is in many ways not as complicated as we often think and has been around for quite some time. An abacus is one of the oldest types of counting devices that you may be familiar with, but ancient and medieval peoples used other devices as well.

For example, taxes in the Middle Ages were usually recorded with notches on a "tally" stick, and other, slightly more complicated devices such as the slide rule began circulating in the 1600s. By the late 1800s and early 1900s, a number of mechanical counting devices had been invented, which looked closer to what we would consider a "computer." Still, the first true computer wasn't invented until the 1930s.

Although, if you saw one of the first computers, you probably wouldn't know it was a computer. It didn't have a screen and was just a bunch of boards, bulbs, and wires!

Alan Turing is sometimes thought of as the father of the modern computer because of his 1936 publication, *On Computable Numbers*, which outlined the ideas of programmable instructions and stored programs.

But computer technology moved relatively slow and had to wait for other advances in transistor and chip technology that were being made in Silicon Valley in the 1950s and '60s. Yes, Silicon Valley was a major tech hub even back then, which brings us to our next important event in modern world history.

On April 1, 1976, Steve Jobs, Steve Wozniak, and Ronald Wayne (who's he?) started the Apple Computer Company in the garage of Jobs' parents' home in Los Altos, California. They took the name from the story of Newton and the apple tree (remember that?). The two Steve's had come a long way from when they first met five years prior. Wozniak was 21 at the time and a hacker who sold "blue boxes" - devices that could be used to make free long distance calls, from anywhere to anywhere - while Jobs was a 16-year-old kid who although precocious, didn't have much direction in his life.

By the mid-1970s, Jobs and Wozniak were college dropouts who spent most of their time tinkering with the mammoth computers that were available at the time. Wozniak knew that he could develop a computer that was more accessible and easier for the average person to use than what was on the market, so he designed his own and tried to sell the idea to Hewlett Packard.

HP turned Wozniak down, but Jobs liked the idea, so the two decided to start their own business.

You're probably wondering, "what about that other guy?"

Ronald Wayne was their older, more experienced friend who worked at Atari at the time. Just two weeks after helping the two Steve's start their new venture, Apple, and being given a 10% share, he sold that share for $800.

Talk about a blunder!

But that's a topic for another book.

Jobs and Wozniak began selling their Apple I computer in July 1976, and it was immediately clear to anyone in the tech industry that they were on to something big. The computer used a TV as a display screen, which was new for computers at the time, had a cassette deck for loading programs, and a simple booting method that those unfamiliar with computers could easily learn.

The Apple II came out a year later and became the standard for home computers. By the 1980s, as home computers became more affordable and integrated into our society, other brands, including HP, were heavily influenced by Apple's technology and style.

If computers had a lineage, all computers today could trace theirs back to the Apple I and Apple II in one form or another.

Truly, Apple made computers affordable and easy to use for *billions* of people around the world. But Apple's role in the lower cost of computers is another part of the major influence the company has had on modern history.

Apple is not just a technology success story, but also a business success.

Today, Apple's revenue totals more than $365 billion, selling the fourth-most computers by numbers worldwide, and is the number two phone manufacturer in the world. Apple's success is driven by a combination of quality, affordability, and hip marketing that creates brand identity and loyalty.

Plus, it has recently made the jump into streaming services and original content.

If you had to name the most important company/corporation in the world today - socially, culturally, economically, and politically - Apple Inc. would probably be at the top of most lists.

It's pretty incredible when you think how it all started with a couple of nerds in their parents' garage.

WHERE'S AFGHANISTAN?

On Christmas Eve Day 1979, few people in the world probably could've answered that question. And when I say, "in the world," I truly mean throughout the world, not just the often geographically-challenged United States. This is nothing against Afghanistan, just that it's a historically small country that's sandwiched between some larger, more powerful ones: Russia, China, India, and Iran.

Afghanistan doesn't have many natural resources worth getting excited about and it's a bit isolated; it's landlocked and covered in rugged mountains and unforgiving deserts. And the Afghan people have historically been averse to outsiders telling them what to do.

Afghanistan was known as Bactria in the ancient and medieval eras and although the Achaemenid Persians listed it as one of their colonies in the 6th century BCE, it was often in rebellion.

Bactria later proved to be troublesome for other conquerors who attempted to control it as well, from Alexander the Great to the Mughals. The Bactrian people valued their independence above all else.

By the 1700s, Bactria had been given its modern name, Afghanistan, but little had changed: the people were still fiercely independent, and the land was fairly isolated. The British invaded Afghanistan twice (1839-1842) and (1878-1880), with limited results, in order to check the Russian imperial advance.

Afghanistan is one of Russia's (in 1979, it was still the Soviet Union) central Asian neighbors to the south, so although the landlocked country doesn't offer much in resources, it provides a strategic location for Russian access to oil-rich Iran and its enemy China.

If you'll remember, although the Soviet Union/Russia and China were both communist, by the mid-1960s, they had grown apart and by the late '60s, they were pretty much enemies, with some shootings happening along their shared border in 1968.

So, by late 1979, Soviet leader Leonid Brezhnev had his eyes on China just as much as he did the US. After all, the 1970s was the era of détente in Soviet-American Cold War relations, so he didn't want to ruffle too many feathers.

But it was the Cold War, after all, so Brezhnev still did whatever he could to spread the interests of the Soviet Union around the world, beginning in the USSR's backyard with Afghanistan.

Afghanistan's modern government was habitually corrupt and generally hated by most of the people, so when it was overthrown in 1978, it wasn't much of a shock to the world. What was a bit shocking, though, was that the government that came to power was a pro-Soviet communist dictatorship (maybe not too shocking, considering its proximity to the Soviet Union)!

Well, the very traditional, very Muslim people of Afghanistan, especially those in the more rural areas, quickly hated the new government, which they saw as godless and authoritarian, as much as the old one.

Seeing an opportunity, the US and Pakistan began supporting the Afghan rebels, known as the mujahideen, against the communist Afghan government.

The Soviets at first sent a few military advisors and intelligence officers to support the Afghan government (sound familiar?), but they finally decided to go with a full invasion on December 24, 1979.

It was a decision that had so many implications in history that we haven't even realized all of them yet.

The immediate effect was felt across Afghanistan and the Soviet Union, as the Red Army quickly learned that defeating a bunch of medieval tribesmen was much easier said than done.

Internationally, the Americans quickly jumped on the situation to point out Soviet hypocrisy, noting that the Soviets are also quick to point out American or Western "imperialism," but there they were doing the same thing.

The United States led a boycott of the 1980 Summer Olympics in Moscow, Soviet Union, which was followed by 65 other countries, making it the least attended games since 1956. Among the notable countries to join the American-led boycott were Canada, West Germany, Argentina, China, Japan, South Korea, and Iran, but interestingly most other NATO countries, including Britain, decided to attend.

But the United States also took a more direct approach to the Soviet-Afghan War.

The CIA became heavily involved with the Pakistani intelligence agency, ISI, to logistically support the mujahedeen, and, later, to directly funnel them weapons. The operations may have helped the mujahedeen defeat the Soviets, but they also destabilized

Pakistan's government, leading to the rise of extremism in that country.

The CIA's involvement in the Soviet-Afghan War gave the maligned agency a renewed vigor. After revelations of many of the CIA's more nefarious projects were made public in the 1970s - such as Operation CHAOS and Operation Midnight Climax, just to name two - the Agency had lost some prestige, funding, and possibly power (although the last one is difficult to say due to the organization's secretive nature). After the Soviet-Afghan War, the CIA rose to its prominent position atop the "deep state," and some would say that it is even more powerful today than ever.

The influence of mujahedeen fighters was another interesting scenario that the CIA didn't anticipate, or maybe they did. The terrorists involved in the 1993 World Trade Center Bombing in New York were former mujahedeen and after another group of terrorists finished the job in 2001, it was revealed their leaders, Osama bin Laden and Khalid Sheikh Muhammad were also former mujahedeen.

Those are all pretty big consequences, but what about the Soviet Union?

Many people have called Afghanistan, "Russia's Vietnam" due to the nature of the fighting and its unwinnable nature. The Soviets tried the "hearts and minds" approach and when that didn't work, they resorted to brutality, but as always is the case, when an occupying force starts killing innocent civilians, they've already lost the war.

Soviet leader Mikhail Gorbachev realized this and finally brought all the Soviet troops home. By the time the last Soviet soldier left Afghanistan on February 15, 1989, the Soviets had suffered 14,453 deaths at the hands of the mujahedeen. More than 50,000 Soviet soldiers were injured, many of them permanently.

It was the Soviet military's greatest loss of life since World War II.

The Soviet-Afghan War caused great divisions in the Soviet Union between the elites and the majority of the population, although due to the nature of the totalitarian regime, the people weren't able to express their feelings, legally.

The Soviet-Afghan War also decimated the Soviet Union's economy, which was not equipped to handle a long, drawn-out war. The US, on the other hand, was prospering economically in the 1980s and could afford to send almost limitless amounts of weapons to the mujahadeen. And due to a combination of a strong economy and a much more politically conservative population at the time, most Americans had no problem sending arms and money to Afghanistan to "fight the Russkies."

Some historians and economists point to December 24, 1979, as being the beginning of the end of the Soviet Union. When you consider the big picture consequences of the Soviet invasion of Afghanistan, it makes you wonder what the Americans were thinking by being there so long.

Sometimes history really does repeat itself!

"MR. GORBACHEV, TEAR DOWN THIS WALL!"

On June 12, 1987, American President Ronald Reagan stood in front of the Berlin Wall and gave what became an iconic speech to the people of West Berlin. In some ways, it echoed President Kennedy's famous "Ich bin ein Berliner" speech on June 26, 1963, nearly two years after the Wall had first been built, but it was different on so many levels.

For one thing, Kennedy's speech was directed at the people of West Berlin, who felt like they were under siege by East Germany and the Soviet Union. Reagan's speech, though, was directed at Soviet leader Mikhail Gorbachev who came to power in 1985 as a reformer.

Gorbachev knew that the Soviet system was living on borrowed time, so he attempted a policy of restructuring the government and the Communist Party (perestroika) and more openness to the West as well as less censorship and repression domestically (glasnost).

Glasnost ended up being a success while perestroika was much less so. In fact, Gorbachev's reforms led to pro-democracy movements forming throughout East Europe.

So, Reagan's speech was basically a call to Gorbachev and the other Eastern European leaders to speed the process up a bit.

Reagan's speech represented a fundamental shift in world geopolitics that was taking place in the communist bloc that few people in the West were truly aware of at the time. Although Reagan's speech didn't get much attention back then, but about two-and-a-half years later, it garnered plenty of attention when the world was shocked by *the* event of the 1980s.

Changes had long been simmering throughout the 1980s in Eastern Europe, beginning with the Polish anti-communist Solidarity movement. Finally, after years of struggle, Solidarity won, when Poland dissolved its communist government in September 1989 and moved toward free elections in 1990.

Then came Hungary, where communism was never very popular. The Hungarian people violently opposed the Soviet Union in a failed 1956 revolution, so when the Hungarian government announced in October 1989 that it would have free elections in early 1990, the people of the nation celebrated in the streets.

But the biggest event in the fall of Eastern European communism took place on November 9, 1989, when the Berlin Wall finally came crashing down.

The process behind the Fall of the Berlin Wall had already been well underway when Reagan visited the city more than two years earlier, so when it finally did happen, it was peaceful and resembled more an outdoor concert than a revolution.

In fact, American David Hasselhoff (yes, *the* Hasselhoff from *Baywatch* and *Knight Rider* fame) even did an impromptu concert on top the Wall. Suddenly, Germans could once again travel back and forth between East and West, allowing family members

198

who hadn't seen each other in years, or even decades, to rekindle their relationships.

Then, on October 3, 1990, Germany was officially reunified.

Czechoslovakia then followed. For those of you under the age of 35, Czechoslovakia was the name of a communist country that combined the Czech Republic and Slovakia. After communism ended, those two countries once again became independent.

Bulgaria relatively peacefully transitioned to democracy next, with Romania seeing a bit more violence, at least for its rulers, and Yugoslavia descended into ethnic warfare that lasted throughout most of the 1990s.

You're probably wondering how the Soviet Union was affected by all this?

Well, this is where some irony comes into play. Gorbachev never really wanted to end the Soviet Union, just reform so it could survive, but the reforms he made really only made the collapse of the system happen that much quicker. Once the people got a taste of the "other side," there was no going back.

And once the technically independent countries of Eastern Europe became independent, it was only a matter of time before the Soviet "republics" did as well.

The truth is, the Soviet Union was little more than a revamped Russian empire with a veneer of communist propaganda. The other "republics" that comprised the Soviet Union never wanted to be part of it, so when the people of the Eastern European countries demanded democracy, the people of the Soviet republics followed their lead.

Lithuania, Latvia, Estonia, Armenia, Moldova, Georgia, and the other central Asian republics left the Soviet Union in 1990. Threats were made and Soviet troops briefly entered the Baltic countries in 1991, but heavy violence was averted.

Communist hardliners also tried to remove reformer Boris Yeltsin from power in Russia in August 1991, but by then it was too late. The people had spoken and they were done with communism and totalitarian governments in Eastern Europe, at least for a while. The Soviet Union officially ended on December 26, 1991, ending the Cold War.

The whirlwind of protest and pro-democracy movements in Eastern Europe may have begun in Poland in the early 1980s, but it kicked into high gear on November 9, 1989, with David Hasselhoff doing a number on the remains of the Berlin Wall.

NO ONE SAW IT COMING

Economist and philosopher Nassim Nicholas Taleb first articulated the idea of what he called a "black swan event" in his 2007 best-selling book, *The Black Swan: The Impact of the Highly Improbable*. Taleb argued that no one thinks of these types of events until they happen, and once they do happen, they often change history and sometimes even create a paradigm shift.

If you look at our book, most, if not all of the stories we've covered so far could probably be considered black swan events. The discovery of gold in California and diamonds in South Africa were certainly black swan events. The Pilgrims landing at Plymouth instead of Virginia was also a true black swan, as were the events that ended the Cold War.

But perhaps the greatest black swan event covered in this book, and the one that is still fresh in many of our minds is the 9-11 Attacks.

On that warm late summer day, 19 Islamic militants hijacked three passenger planes, crashing one into the World Trade Center towers in New York City, destroying them, another into the Pentagon in Washington, DC, while heroic passengers resisted the hijackers on a third flight, bringing it down in a field in rural Pennsylvania.

Chances are, you still clearly remember what you were doing on that day and the range of emotions you felt.

The terrorists killed nearly 3,000 people and caused more than $10 billion in damage in what remains the worst terrorist attack in world history. Since the attacks were so shocking and unexpected, and because they caused so much damage, the effects were massive and still felt today.

The US government and military immediately went to war, although it was never quite clear who they were fighting. Since the mastermind of the 9-11 Attacks, Osama bin Laden, was hiding in Afghanistan, an international military coalition led by the US attacked and occupied that country.

But we remember how well that worked for the Soviet Union, right?

By the time the Afghanistan War finally ended in August 2021, 3,576 coalition force members had been killed, 2,240 of which were Americans. And like the Soviet-Afghan War, the Afghanistan War has driven a wedge between people in Western countries like few other issues. If you searched for sources of the recent political polarization in many Western countries, especially the US, the Afghanistan War would definitely be one.

Then there were the weapons of mass destruction.

For reasons that remain unknown, and which provide plenty of grist for conspiracy theories, Iraq's dictator at the time, Saddam Hussein, was accused by the CIA and members of the US government of somehow being connected to the 9-11 Attacks and also stocking "weapons of mass destruction."

Neither of those were true, but it didn't prevent a US-led invasion of Iraq that was even costlier than the Afghanistan War. Nearly 5,000 coalition soldiers were killed, 4,507 Americans, in the war that lasted from 2003 to 2014. The Iraq War was even more domestically polarizing than the Afghanistan War.

The immediate reaction to 9-11 in the US may have been more American flags hanging from doorways and porches than ever before, and a temporary sense of unity, but within a year, that unity had dissolved into even more political and social division.

The 9-11 Attacks also led to wide-ranging surveillance of American citizens under the Patriot Act, which despite these wars being ended, has only been strengthened.

WHAT HAPPENED WHEN THE HOUSING MARKET BUBBLE POPPED?

For our final entry of very important events that changed modern history, we go back just a decade or so to 2007-2008 to look at another case of history repeating itself - to a certain extent.

The early 2000s began well enough for most people. Although the 9-11 Attacks shook people around the world, they were never followed up with other major attacks, so by late 2002, people were once again going about their business.

And in the early 2000s, the stock market was up, interest rates were down, and so too were prices of homes. Many people were buying homes up with cash and those who didn't have the cash readily available faced few problems getting a loan.

Loans were being given out like candy in the early 2000s. Sound familiar?

Well, it should, because just like the stock market bubble that popped and crashed in 1929, the United States was on the threshold of something similar in 2007.

In the years leading up to 2007, Americans were rightfully taking advantage of low home prices and easy credit to buy homes at a rate never seen in history. Many of the loans home buyers received were so-called "subprime loans," which are often given to people with less than average credit at much higher rates.

The subprime mortgage problem probably wouldn't have been so bad if it happened in isolation, but in 2007, isolation was a thing of the past. Every element of the American economy is connected and integrated with the other parts, and the American economy is integrated and connected with all the national economies throughout the world.

When things go south in the USA, things will go bad everywhere.

Numerous multinational corporations, banks, and trading firms were heavily invested in the US housing market, so when homeowners began defaulting on their loans in significant numbers in late 2007, it created a ripple effect throughout the global economy and political systems.

Almost immediately some of the biggest multinational national corporations were in danger of going under. Many well-known and influential investment companies, such as Bear Stearns, did go under in 2008. The year 2008 was a bloodbath for major banks and investment companies, with the peak of the bankruptcies taking place on September 15, 2008, when long-time investment company Lehman Brothers called it quits.

At that point, the government got involved by bailing out some corporations, which trickled down to some homeowners. Unfortunately, by then the damage had been done, and the world was officially in what became known as the Great Recession.

As the Great Recession gained steam, unemployment rates picked up, going above 10% in several countries for 2009 and most of 2010 before decreasing again.

One of the major political effects of the Great Recession was the 2008 presidential election in the United States. Then,Senator Barak Obama from Illinois swept into the White House on a campaign of reform and change, becoming the country's first Black president.

The economy limped on, and Obama was blamed by many for not doing more, which some say led to the election of Donald Trump in 2016.

But not every country was hurt by the Great Recession.

Interestingly, most of the countries in the Southern Hemisphere actually did well and their economies grew during the Great Recession. China, India, Brazil, Australia, and most African countries' economies grew during the Great Recession, while nearly every country in the latitudes north of China suffered.

CONCLUSION

I hope you enjoyed *The Encyclopedia of Very Important Events through Modern History* and the trip we took through time. Since there is something for everyone in this book, I'm sure you learned at least a thing or two from one of the book's 54 stories and had a little fun in the process. And as you've got to the end of this book, I'm sure you're wondering why an important event or two were left out, right?

I'm sure you can think of some important, history-changing events yourself. I'll be the first one to tell you that many more events can be added to these 54. I guess that gives you something to think about, which is, after all, the whole point of learning. Just as each of the major events in this book affected later events, which then affected more events, creating a ripple effect of important events, the facts you learned in this book will lead to you learning new things.

You'll also be able to start seeing the world a little differently after reading this book.

Now when you hear about an important event in the news, the buildup of troops in Ukraine in early 2022, for instance, you'll know that they didn't just arrive at that event overnight and for no reason. In the case of Ukraine, well, it was recently part of the Soviet Union, so Russia has an ongoing interest in the region.

Also, you now know that any outside attempt to invade it could very well end as it did for Napoleon!

Truly, world history is the culmination of major events that have rippled throughout the world and will continue to do so as long as humans exist. Who knows, the next major event may be happening right now, and we won't even know its impact for many years.